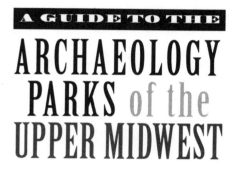

A GUIDE TO THE

ARCHAEOLOGY PARKS of the UPPER MIDWEST

A GUIDE TO THE
ARCHAEOLOGY
PARKS of the
UPPER MIDWEST

Deborah Morse-Kahn

ROBERTS
RINEHART

Published by Roberts Rinehart Publishers
An imprint of the Rowman & Littlefield Publishing Group, Inc.
4501 Forbes Boulevard, Suite 200
Lanham, MD 20706

Distributed by National Book Network

Book design: Barbara Werden Design

Library of Congress Cataloging-in-Publication Data

Morse-Kahn, Deborah, 1952–
    A guide to the archaeology parks of the upper Midwest / Deborah Morse-Kahn.
        p.   cm.
    Includes bibliographical references and index.
    ISBN 1-57098-396-8 (alk. paper)
    1. Indians of North America—Middle West—Antiquities—Guidebooks.
    2. Archaeological parks—Middle West—Guidebooks. 3. Middle West—Antiquities—Guidebooks. I. Title.
    E78.M67M67 2003
    977'.01—dc21
                                                            2003002129

Manufactured in the United States of America.

*For Barbara, She-Who-Walks-Like-Deer,
who first took me up into the sandstone bluffs above the
Mississippi to show me the wonders there.*

*For John, without whom there would have been
neither vision nor understanding.*

CONTENTS

ACKNOWLEDGMENTS

Many Upper Midwest colleagues helped guide the research for this book: Bob Birmingham, State Archaeologist for Wisconsin; Bill Green, a past State Archaeologist for Iowa and now the director of the Logan Museum of Anthropology, Beloit College, Wisconsin; Scott Anfinson, National Register Archaeologist for the State Historic Preservation Office, Minnesota; Robert "Ernie" Boszhardt, Regional Archaeologist for the Mississippi Valley Archaeology Center at the University of Wisconsin–La Crosse; Lori Stanley, Faculty in Anthropology at Luther College in Decorah, Iowa; and Thomas F. King, Cultural Resource Specialist, of Washington, D.C.

Rick Rinehart of Roberts Rinehart Publishers showed great patience in the publishing process, and Mitch Allen of AltaMira Press has my gratitude for his encouragement and support.

Special thanks go to Wisconsin's Rock River Archaeological Society and Friends of Horicon Marsh for first sponsoring programming on regional archaeology sites and for showing such enthusiasm for this publication. Robert Salzer, Anthropology Professor Emeritus of Beloit College and the now retired director of the Logan Museum of Anthropology, provided me the model of deep respect, sense of wonder, and generosity of spirit that has helped me approach this effort in the proper frame of mind.

Barbara Bloom Gittens of Caledonia, Minnesota, was my first guide into the world of the Upper Midwest's prehistoric places many years ago, and a more able tracker amid woodland and bluffland I have never met. John F. Campbell of Milwaukee, Wisconsin, has been my tutor, guide, and happy surveying companion over the past decade and deserves all my thanks.

PREFACE: HOW TO
USE THIS BOOK

Each archaeology park has been assigned a number that can be used to find the site on the map and in the book chapters. The list that follows provides the assigned number, the state acronym, the park name, and, where helpful for understanding location, the nearest community to the park.

The first chapters in the book talk about the reasons we go on pilgrimage to archaeology parks; a brief overview of the prehistory of the region and the special symbolism of the effigy mounds and rock art found here; and then a consideration on traveling thoughtfully to these unusual heritage tourism destinations. The chapters on the parks follow; they are grouped by district, with local agency and chamber of commerce contacts provided, to permit easy travel planning. A list of helpful state historic and tourism information contacts follows, as does a brief list of additional reading on Upper Midwest archaeology. Finally, a list of all the parks by state precedes the index.

New archaeology park sites are developed every year as communities partner with state agencies and tribal nations to protect and interpret the cultural treasures in their midst. I welcome all communications concerning these new parks, corrections to the current listings, and any thoughts and ideas you may have concerning this guidebook and its uses.

DEBORAH MORSE-KAHN, M.A.

Director
Regional Research Associates
Minneapolis, MN USA
dmorsekahn@mn.rr.com

NUMBERED PARK SITES

NORTHERN MINNESOTA AND THE RAINY RIVER

1 MN—Grand Mound, near International Falls
2 ON—Kay Nah Chi Wah Nung, near Rainy River

CENTRAL MINNESOTA AND THE LAKES REGION

3 MN—Cut Foot Sioux Trail, Chippewa National Forest
4 MN—Winnibigoshish Lake Dam, Chippewa National Forest
5 MN—Itasca State Park
6 MN—Gull Lake Dam
7 MN—Mille Lacs Kathio State Park

MINNEAPOLIS–ST. PAUL AND THE METROPOLITAN AREA

8 MN—Indian Mounds Regional Park, St. Paul
9 MN—Mounds Springs Park, Minnesota Valley National Wildlife Refuge, Bloomington
10 MN—Historic Murphy's Landing, Minnesota Valley National Wildlife Refuge, near Shakopee

11 MN—Memorial Park, Shakopee

12 WI—Birkmose Park, Hudson

The Day Trips

13 MN—Red Wing Archaeological Preserve, Cannon
Valley Trail, Red Wing

14 WI—Bird (or Bow and Arrow) Petroform, near Hager
City

15 WI—Indian Burial Ground, near Spooner

16 WI—Indian Mounds Park, Rice Lake

17 WI—Wakanda Park, Menomonie

MINNESOTA'S SOUTHWEST PLAINS

18 MN—Jeffers Petroglyphs

19 MN—Pipestone National Monument

THE DRIFTLESS AREA

20 WI—Perrot State Park, near Trempealeau

21 WI—Myrick Park, La Crosse

22 WI—Riverside Cemetery, near Genoa

23 IA—Fish Farm Mounds State Preserve, near New
Albin

24 IA—Slinde Mounds State Preserve, near Hanover

25 IA—Effigy Mounds National Monument, near
Marquette

26 IA—Pike's Peak State Park, near McGregor

27 WI—Wyalusing State Park, near Prairie du Chien

28 WI—Nelson Dewey State Park

29 IA—Turkey River Mounds State Preserve

DUBUQUE AND POINTS SOUTH

30 IA—Little Maquoketa River Mounds State Preserve,
    near Dubuque
31 IA—Catfish Creek State Preserve, Mines of Spain
    Recreation Area, near Dubuque
32 IA—Bellevue State Park
33 IA—Wickiup Hill Outdoor Learning Center, near
    Cedar Rapids
34 IA—Indian Fish Trap State Preserve, near Amana
35 IA—Toolesboro Mounds State Preserve
36 IA—James Weed Park, Muscatine
37 IL—Albany Mounds State Historic Site

WEST OF CHICAGO

38 IL—Briscoe Mounds, near Channahon
39 IL—Oakwood Cemetery, Joliet
40 IL—Higginbotham Woods Forest Preserve, Joliet
41 IL—Winfield Mounds Forest Preserve
42 IL—Beattie Park Mounds, Rockford

MILWAUKEE AND THE LOWER ROCK RIVER

43 WI—Beloit College Mounds
44 WI—Mound Cemetery, Racine
45 WI—Indian Mounds Park, Whitewater
46 WI—Carroll College Mounds, Waukesha
47 WI—Cutler Park, Waukesha
48 WI—Jefferson County Indian Mounds and Trail Park,
    Koshkonong Mounds Country Club, near Fort
    Atkinson

54 WI—Wisconsin Heights Battle Site, near Sauk City

55 WI—Devil's Lake State Park, near Baraboo

56 WI—Man Mound County Park, near Baraboo

57 WI—Kingsley Bend Mounds, near Wisconsin Dells

58 WI—Gee's Slough (New Lisbon) Mounds

59 WI—Cranberry Creek Mound Group, near Necedah

60 WI—Roche-A-Cri State Park, near Friendship

61 WI—Whistler Indian Mounds Park, Hancock

62 WI—Upper Whiting Park

63 WI—Lake Emily County Park, Amherst Junction

FOUR RIVERS AND POINTS NORTH

64 WI—Lizard Mounds County Park, near West Bend

65 WI—Horicon Marsh, near Mayville

66 WI—Indian Mounds Park, Sheboygan

67 WI—Henschel Homestead/Museum of Indian History, near Elkhart Lake

68 WI—Calumet County Park, near Stockbridge

69 WI—High Cliff State Park, near Sherwood

70 WI—Toft Point, near Bailey's Harbor

71 WI—Washington Island Mounds

72 WI—Copper Culture State Park and Museum, Oconto

73 MI—Adventure Copper Mine, Greenland

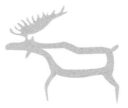

The Archaeology Parks of the Upper Midwest

What is an archaeology park? An archaeology park can have many definitions for the purposes of this guidebook:

- an archaeological site enclosed by specific boundaries and open to the public, such as the Jeffers Petroglyphs in southwestern Minnesota
- a parkland offering recreational facilities in which can also be found interpreted archaeology sites that are a valued part of the park plan, such as the many state parks in Wisconsin that contain effigy mounds
- a public place in which may be found remnants of prehistoric cultures, such as Mound Cemetery in Racine, which intentionally shelters and preserves both prehistoric burial mounds and Wisconsin pioneer gravesites

The Upper Midwest—Minnesota, eastern Iowa, northwestern Illinois, and Wisconsin—contains a wealth of all three types of archaeology parks, sheltering much of the known remnants of those prehistoric cultures in our region. For this guidebook, the focus will indeed be solely on prehistory and on the unique cultures that passed through these four states.

For us in the Upper Midwest, this means especially the Effigy Mound culture that left behind the spectacular symbolic earthworks that cover much of our region. And in many places the symbology expanded in use for what today we call rock art—petroglyphs (carvings) and pictographs (paintings). Often nearby or among these forms are the burial mounds, some small and some enormous, all of great ceremonial significance.

The archaeology parks of the Upper Midwest are small enchantments, a chance to knowingly stand where others stood one thousand or more years ago, to consider how they lived and died and what the world may have been like in their time. The parks also educate us to the vital cultures of ancient peoples and to the living inheritances of those cultures among the tribal nations that hold the earlier civilizations as their own. And, finally, we can consider our common ground with others, the use of familiar and primary symbolism of our human nature, and the need to connect to earth and water, air and fire; to ensure shelter, food, warmth, and safety; and to bless the ground under our feet and praise the stars in the sky. We are not, after all, so different today.

CHAPTER 1

The Ancient Peoples

The Upper Midwest—for our purposes all of Minnesota, eastern Iowa, northwestern Illinois, and all of Wisconsin—has seen human habitation for over twelve thousand years, since not long after the glaciers retreated. Modern scholars term this postglacial era the Paleo-Indian era (roughly from 10,000 to 6500 B.C.E.), a time of mastodons and woolly mammoths. Though we have little evidence of the people who lived then, we know that they made tools, gathered vegetation for food and for healing, and lived in large extended families that traded widely with other groups.

In the Early, Middle, and Late Archaic eras the hunting districts of these groups became more settled, and efforts to raise crops are known to have begun some time around 3000 B.C.E. We know that, over the ensuing era, ceremony and ritual began to surround the most basic of human functions, including birth, death, and the gathering and raising of food. Burial mound building is evidence of this increased attention to ritual.

It is known that small round and conical burial mounds

first appeared in Wisconsin during the Early Woodland phase, dated from 800 B.C.E. to as late as 100 C.E. This group was the first to use pottery for cooking and the storing of grains, to collect wild grasses and nuts, to cultivate some crops, and to establish semipermanent territorial camps in season for hunting and fishing.

The Middle Woodland era (100 B.C.E. to about 500 c.e.) saw an increase in mound building, and those who lived then began to build much larger mounds and to set them in groups, employing rock, ash, clays, and special soils that would have provided protection for the rebirth of the soul. Sometimes only one body was buried in the depth of the mounds; sometimes many were interred.

The Late Woodland era (from 650 B.C.E. to about 1200 c.e.) saw a tremendous increase in mound building, influenced to some extent by more complex societies, the Hopewell and Mississippian cultures, in the south along the Mississippi River, who traded with the Woodland people. Mounds were often raised near village sites where permanent crop fields were established. It was during this era, also, that the Oneota, an agricultural group, flourished after 1000 c.e., primarily in what is now present-day Wisconsin.

A spectacular outcome of the Late Woodland culture was effigy mound building, using earthen piles to create animal and geometric forms, often in mixed groups, and placed on high levels above water. Several schools of thought exist about the meaning of the mounds, the most common now being the representation of clans tied to elements: Earth, Water, and Air. The animal forms especially can be tied to ancient legends of spirit beings, and many of the mound groups are now considered to be celestial markers as well. The effigy mounds do at times contain burials, though not always.

These effigies, generally built in the time between 650 and 1200 C.E., reflect recurrent themes that can be seen in the many archaeological parks that today shelter the few remaining effigy mounds that escaped destruction by plow or development since European settlement in the Upper Midwest: Panther (Water Spirit), Thunderbird, Turtle (or Lizard), Bear, Deer, Snake, Human, Linear, Oval, and Conical. The many rock art (petroglyph and pictograph) sites known throughout the Upper Midwest, which span many of the above-mentioned eras, also carry many of these same symbols, plus the classic celestial symbols of sun, moon, and stars. Other common rock art motifs are spears (atlatls), hands, birds' feet (turkey tracks), shields, and the underworld.

The first European settlers arrived just five hundred years after the end of the effigy mound era, a mere heartbeat in time, and the interest in these "antiquities," which we know to be the last vestiges of a living culture, began in earnest. By the early 1800s surveyors were making notes and sketches of the mounds and the rock carvings, and formal commissioned surveys began in the 1850s. We are, in our time, indebted to the efforts of these skilled engineers—in particular T. H. Lewis, Increase Lapham, and Jacob Brower—for highly detailed drawings and maps of mound and rock art sites that have long been lost to modern development.

Today's Ho-Chunk (Winnebago), Dakota (Sioux), Ojibwe, and Iowa tribal nations have long cultural memories of the meaning and sacredness of these sites and may truly be considered the modern inheritors of these ancient peoples. It is with their support and their generosity that we can know so much about the meaning and place of the effigies and carvings of another people long departed and, combined with the considerable skills and the new sensibilities of archaeologists, sociologists, and ethnographers, that we find ourselves the collective inheritors of a great culture past.

CHAPTER 2

Heritage Tourists, Privileged Travelers

Visiting archaeology parks, indeed, any kind of site or museum associated with the stories of people long past, is a passion for many of us who love both history and prehistory. The archaeology parks, unlike any other park site or exhibit we are likely to encounter, pose some special issues in self-education and in conduct.

AS IT ONCE WAS

The old world of archaeological research into the visible vestiges of ancient cultures—particularly the old methods of excavation and collecting human remains and artifacts—is now thankfully past. Mounds are no longer opened, out of respect for the dead and for the cultural rights and sensibilities of today's tribal nations. We would no more open the grave of those dead one thousand years ago than we would permit strangers to open the graves of our own families. Desecration ("pot hunting") in burial and effigy mounds is punishable under federal law, and rightly so, and those human remains and sacred objects held for more than a century by local, regional, and national museums are being returned to the tribal nations through a system devised under the Native American Graves Protection and Repatriation Act (NAGPRA).

There are new technologies and sensibilities also involved in the study of the beautiful carvings and paintings found on rock surfaces throughout the Upper Midwest. Where rock art was once virtually ignored except by ethnologists, now these stunning symbols of ceremony and seasons are being sheltered where possible and thoughtfully interpreted to better understand ancient cultures. And the methods by which we study them have also changed drastically: not only are the old techniques of chalking or glazing to bring out the carved relief wholly unacceptable by today's standards, now the rock surface goes virtually untouched as new dating and lighting methods are used to examine the rock face.

TRAVELING KINDLY

"Teach your children well. . . ." Crosby, Stills, and Nash had it right when they wrote this. Traveling to archaeology parks to study the effigy and burial mounds, rock art, and ancient village sites of prehistoric peoples asks a new sensibility, even a sense of awe, as we stand where others once stood so long ago. Great ceremony was involved in even the smallest aspects of daily living for those who were so tied to earth, sky, and water.

Help your children understand what they are seeing, show them what is special about these places, and give them books to read that will teach them about what they are going to see, or have just seen, and about the cultures of today's tribal nations, which have been strong partners in the restoration and protection of these sacred places. I know of a family who, in the tradition of many Native Americans, never departs from an effigy mound or burial site without leaving a tiny bundle of leaves and tobacco as a gratitude offering. Such small gestures tie us to those who have now passed in a way nothing else can.

WHEN AND HOW TO TRAVEL

It is in the nature of effigy and burial mound sites that, once covered with snow, they cannot be seen! It is a small point but one necessary to make right from the outset. Beyond that, the times of the year when there is little or no leaf-out—spring and late autumn—are ideal to most clearly see the detail of the mounds. Do remember that many of the state parks are open to hunters for specific periods of time in the autumn, so contact the park office or the state tourism divisions using the phone numbers or e-mail addresses provided in this book before you set out.

Finally, the issue of accessibility for those with movement disabilities is a tough one. These archaeology sites, by their very nature, are often reachable only over unpaved paths, atop hills and ridges, or deep in untracked woodland. Where park sites can offer a comfortably accessible chance to view mounds or rock art, I have taken care to say so.

CHAPTER 3

Northern Minnesota and the Rainy River

The Rainy River forms the border between Minnesota and Ontario, in the district we know as Voyageurs National Park, and this region has been home to humans for over ten thousand years. Those civilizations dwelling in this region left countless large and small burial mounds as evidence of their social and religious culture. Though a great many of the mounds have been destroyed since the time of European settlement, two important burial mound sites still exist and are carefully interpreted for the public as parklands.

(1) GRAND MOUND
International Falls, MN

The Grand Mound, on the Rainy River's south shore where the smaller Bigfork River flows north into the Rainy, is the largest prehistoric burial site in the Upper Midwest and Canadian Shield region, built sometime between 200 B.C.E. to 800 C.E. The great mound is 40 feet high and more than 100 feet across at its base.

Though tourists once came by steamboat up the Rainy River to dig for artifacts, the Grand Mound is now a protected site managed by the Minnesota Historical Society. There is an interpretive center offering extensive exhibits, hands-on activities for young people, and an audiovisual program that explains the peoples and the mounds of thousands of years ago. Lectures and special programs are also offered.

A self-guided path leads through old-growth forest from the interpretive center to the Grand Mound. Two miles of nature trails provide pleasant walking activity and picnic spots. Spring and summer also provide wildflower viewing and bird-watching for enthusiasts. The building, trails, and picnic area are all designed for accessibility.

Grand Mound Historic Site

6749 Highway 11

International Falls, MN 56649

218-285-3332

Directions: 17 miles west of International Falls on Minnesota Highway 11.

Hours: Open May through Labor Day.

Admission: Adults, $4.00; senior citizens, $3.00; children aged six–twelve, $2.00. Free for children under age six and Minnesota Historical Society members. Different fees may apply for special events.

Helpful Contacts

International Falls Area Chamber of Commerce

301 Second Avenue

International Falls, MN 56649

218-283-9400 or 800-325-5766

www.intlfalls.org/kwelcome.htm

(2) KAY NAH CHI WAH NUNG (MANITOU MOUNDS)
Emo, Ontario, Canada

The name "Kay Nah Chi Wah Nung" means "place at the long rapids" and was chosen by the Rainy River First Nations community for the site of a history center near the Manitou ("spirit") Mounds, beautifully preserved ceremonial burial mounds on the upper terrace of the river bank and the largest such concentration of mounds in Canada. The district has magnificent natural features, being built on two broad terraces formed long ago by the outwash of Glacial Lake Aggasiz. The rapids never freeze and so have always offered freshwater fishing for those who have lived here as well as a critical pass-through area for mammal and bird migrations.

The Ojibwe people are the stewards and guardians of the Manitou Mounds district and have been living here for several hundred years, a continuing line of North American peoples who came here for trade, ceremony, and subsistence. The Canadian government declared the area a National Historic Site in 1969. The large and very handsome Kay Nah Chi Wah Nung Historical Centre offers year-round displays and exhibits in five galleries, a gift shop specializing in Ojibwe crafts, a restaurant featuring Ojibwe traditional foods, and a state-of-the-art conservation lab with more than ten thousand cultural artifacts in curation. A large sturgeon tank near the entrance serves to remind visitors that this armor-plated fish, unchanged for millions of years, has its critical spawning grounds at the rapids and has been an important food source for those who came here for thousands of years. A visit to the nearby First Nations Sturgeon Hatchery can be arranged by appointment.

A three-kilometer path takes you to the mound sites along the river as well as two village reconstructions; visitors can walk or use golf carts to cover the distance. Birdwatchers will want to watch for warblers, white pelicans, bald eagles, and occasionally golden eagles.

Kay Nah Chi Wah Nung Historical Centre

P.O. Box 100, Shaw Road
Stratton, Ontario P0W 1N0
Canada
807-483-1163
histctre@first-nation.com
www.longsault.com

Directions: Take Highway 11 west from Fort Frances (at International Falls, MN) or east from Rainy River (at Baudette, MN); between Barwick and Stratton, turn at Shaw Road.

Hours: Open Wednesday through Sunday: summer, 10 A.M.–6 P.M.; winter, 10 A.M.–5 P.M.

Admission: Adult, $7.00; senior citizens, $5.00; children, $3.00 (please call ahead for group or special bookings).

Helpful Contacts

Rainy River District Chamber of Commerce
Box 458, Rainy River
Ontario P0W 1L0
Canada
www.rainyriverchamber.ca

Northwestern Ontario Tourism Association

Box 458, Emo

Ontario P0W 1E0

Canada

www.nwota.com

Central Minnesota and the Lakes Region

Central Minnesota is the recreational heart of the Upper Midwest, blessed with thousands of lakes and streams and magnificent forestlands. It is also the home of many of the Upper Midwest's tribal communities, both ancestral homelands and historic settlements, and the Native American peoples are the stewards of the many cultural and archaeological sites that are fostered in parklands throughout the region.

(3) CUT FOOT SIOUX TRAIL, CHIPPEWA NATIONAL FOREST

Cass Lake, MN

The Chippewa National Forest is the first and oldest of the nation's designated national woodlands. Boasting 1.6 million acres wrapped around the northern, eastern, and southern boundaries of the city of Bemidji, the forest contains 160 miles of trails, 700 lakes—including Winnibigoshish, Leech, and Cass, some of the largest in the state—

and 920 miles of rivers and streams, as well as some outstanding examples of National Register historic buildings, including lodges and a Civilian Conservation Corps camp. Virtually every wilderness activity and sport can be experienced here year-round. The Chippewa is home to the largest breeding population of bald eagles in the United States, and over sixty other sensitive or endangered species of plants and animals are found here.

The Cut Foot Sioux Trail, named for a 1748 Dakota–Ojibwe battle, follows the Continental Divide for 22 miles and leads to the Turtle Mound, a Dakota effigy mound some 25 feet wide by 30 feet long constructed circa 1700 below ground ("intaglio") on the shore of Cut Foot Sioux Lake. The Turtle oracle once pointed north to the enemy, the Ojibwe, and later was reversed to the south when the Ojibwe conquered the Dakota. The Turtle effigy is surrounded by a second effigy mound in the shape of a Snake. The effigy is greatly venerated by native peoples today and is held in stewardship by the Leech Lake Band of Ojibwe.

Information and interpretive and hands-on programs are available at the Cut Foot Sioux Visitor Center.

Chippewa National Forest

Route 3, P.O. Box 244

Cass Lake, MN 56633

218-335-8600

www.fs.fed.us/r9/chippewa

Cut Foot Sioux Trailhead and Visitors Center

44623 Highway 46

Deer River, MN 56636

218-246-8233

Directions: Go east from Bemidji or west from Grand Rapids on Highway 2 to Deer River and then 18 miles North on Highway 46.

Hours: Open daily from Memorial Day through Labor Day.

Helpful Contacts

Cass County Visitor Information
www.co.cass.mn.us/index_pages/visiting_index.html

(4) WINNIBIGOSHISH LAKE DAM, CHIPPEWA NATIONAL FOREST

Near Bemidji, MN

The Lake Winnibigoshish Recreation Area is contained within the Chippewa National Forest as a distinct district, offering year-round recreation opportunities amid heavy red pine forests. The dam at the outlet of the lake has been maintained by the U.S. Army Corps of Engineers since 1884.

An 1883 map survey shows the nearby location of an Ojibwe village and numerous prehistoric burial and effigy mounds. A prominent linear mound can still be seen just east of the present-day Corps of Engineers Maintenance Building.

Winnibigoshish Lake Dam

County Highway 9 at the Mississippi River
Campsite reservations: 877-444-6777
Directions: Go east from Bemidji or west from Grand Rapids on Highway 2 to Deer River and then 12 miles north on Highway 46; go left on County Highway 9 for 2 miles to the sign.

(5) ITASCA STATE PARK
Lake Itasca, MN

Beautiful Itasca is Minnesota's oldest state park and one of the oldest in the nation, established in 1891, holding 32,000 acres of pine forest, extensive hiking and biking trails, and more than one hundred lakes including Lake Itasca, the headwaters of the Mississippi River, which begins its 2,552-mile journey to the Gulf of Mexico. In the midst of Itasca's popular and modern camp grounds is evidence of prehistoric campsites, which have yielded extraordinary evidence of a strong bison killing culture dating back 7,000 years, with many artifacts of bison bone and hide found, as well as extensive burial mounds. Interpretive information, archaeological exhibits, and educational programs are available at the Headwaters History Center, and excellent signage is available at the Bison Kill site and at the Itasca Indian Cemetery.

Itasca State Park

HC05, Box 4

Lake Itasca, MN 56470-9702

218-266-2100

Itasca.park@dnearstate.mn.us

www.dnearstate.mn.us/state_parks/itasca/index.html

Directions: Go south 30 miles from Bemidji or north 21 miles from Park Rapids on U.S. Highway 71 to State Highway 200.

Hours: Interpretive center and programs open daily from May through October.

Helpful Contacts

Park Rapids Chamber of Commerce
P.O. Box 249
Park Rapids, MN 56470
218-732-4111 or 800-247-0054
www.parkrapids.com
Bemidji Visitors and Convention Bureau
P.O. Box 66
Bemidji, MN 56619
218-759-0164 or 800-458-2223 ext. 105
gayle@visitbemidji.com
www.visitbemidji.com</add>

(6) GULL LAKE DAM
Near Nisswa, MN

Gull Lake lies in the midst of one of Minnesota's most extensive lake districts and is one of the state's premier recreation destinations. The Gull Lake Dam, built in 1912, is just downstream from the mouth of the Gull River at the southeast end of the lake and is under the management of the U.S. Army Corps of Engineers. Picnic grounds, hiking and interpretive trails, boating and swimming, and campgrounds are available at the Gull Lake Recreation Area for visitors.

On the eastern edge of the grounds are twelve complete and several partial burial mounds remaining from the Woodland culture that established permanent villages in this area between 800 B.C.E. and 900 C.E. An interpretive display provides information for visitors.

Gull Lake Recreation Area/Gull Lake Area Association

Box 102

Nisswa, MN 56468

218-963-2229

Campsite reservations: 877-444-6777

Directions: Go 10 miles north from Brainerd on State Highway 371 and west on County Roads 125/105 to the lake or west from Brainerd on State Highway 210 to Highway 70 north to the lake.

Helpful Contacts

Brainerd Lakes Area Chamber of Commerce

124 North Sixth Street, P.O. Box 356

Brainerd, MN 56401

218-829-2838 or 800-450-2838

info@explorebrainerdlakes.com

www.explorebrainerdlakes.com

(7) MILLE LACS KATHIO STATE PARK

Onamia, MN

Mille Lacs Kathio is one of Minnesota's true archaeology parks, holding nineteen identified sites ranging over four thousand years of human history. The entire park, found on the banks of one of the state's largest lakes, Mille Lacs, has been designated a National Historic Landmark.

European settlers found the Mdewekanton ("Water of the Great Spirit") Dakota people settled here. The Mille Lacs Band of Ojibwe are a significant presence in the region and stewards of the park's rich cultural inheritance. The Mille Lacs Indian Museum, run by the Minnesota Historical Society in cooperation with the Mille Lacs Band, is just up the road from the park.

The park offers many interpretive exhibits and educational programs focusing on its archaeological sites, including a significant number of burial mounds. Interpretive signage is found throughout the park on the hiking trails. Archaeological site (except mounds) excavations continue in the park and are frequently open to the public.

The Mille Lacs Band offers traditional wild ricing demonstrations on Sundays at the park during the summer months. Mille Lacs Kathio offers the usual outstanding range of recreational activities year-round. Cabins and campgrounds are available by reservation.

Mille Lacs Kathio State Park

15066 Kathio State Park Road

Onamia, MN 56359-2207

320-532-3523

www.dnearstate.mn.us/state_parks/mille_lacs_kathio/
    index.html

Directions: Go north from Onamia 10 miles on State Highway 169 and west on County Road 26.

Hours: Open daily year-round (mounds and interpretive sites are open spring through autumn).

Helpful Contacts

Mille Lacs Indian Museum (Minnesota Historical Society)

43411 Odena Drive

Onamia, MN 56359

320-532-3632

millelacs@mnhs.org

www.mnhs.org/places/sites/mlim/index.html

Directions: Go north from Onamia 12 miles on State Highway 169 (2 miles above Mille Lacs Kathio State Park) to the museum on the west shore of lake.

Hours: Open daily from Memorial Day to Labor Day and on weekends in May and October.

Admission: There is a small admission fee.

Minneapolis–St. Paul and the Metropolitan Area

The Twin Cities metro area sits at the confluence of the Mississippi, Minnesota, and St. Croix Rivers and encompasses one of the most beautiful physical regions in the country as well as the traditional homeland of countless prehistoric peoples. This region of pines and hardwood lands, river valleys and lakes, was once rich in rock art (petroglyphs and pictographs) and burial mound districts, but much has been lost in the time following European settlement. We are blessed with thoughtful documentation of these sites by surveyors working through the region at the turn of the century and with careful stewardship of the remaining sites through private, public, and tribal partnerships. The seven local and three regional sites open to the community—all mounds, the rock art lost long ago—represent a broad range of site size and interpretation, but all are worthy of visiting for an understanding of what has been lost and what has been saved.

(8) INDIAN MOUNDS REGIONAL PARK

St. Paul, MN

This extensive park site on the Mississippi River bluffs above the city of St. Paul once held as many as thirty-seven burial mounds built 1,500–2,000 years ago, but many were leveled in the past centuries to make way for roads. Six of the great mounds still remain in one of the city's most popular parks.

The park, established in 1892 on Dayton's Bluff, has been much groomed over the century, and archaeological research into the mounds did take place in the past when such investigations were still considered acceptable. The famous Carver's Cave, long known for detailed petroglyphs, was just below the mounds, though the glyphs are largely destroyed and the cave has been sealed.

Today the mounds are surrounded by wrought-iron railings but are easily approached. Paved trails lead through the park past picnic spots and a pavilion along the bluff top. A commanding view over the river and downtown St. Paul from the Carver's Cave Overlook is a big drawing point. Parking is available at an adjacent lot. The entire park is thoughtfully accessible.

The newly built Science Museum of Minnesota, with its exceptional natural history and anthropology displays and marvelous Omnitheater experience, is just upriver in downtown St. Paul. Don't miss the Mississippi River prehistory exhibit.

Indian Mounds Regional Park

Mounds Boulevard at Earl Avenue

St. Paul, MN 55101

651-266-6400 (St. Paul Parks and Recreation)

Directions: From I-94 take the East 7th Street/Mounds exit and follow Mounds Boulevard; from downtown St. Paul take East 7th Street and connect to Mounds Boulevard; from Minnehaha Avenue connect to Johnson Parkway, south to the park.

Hours: Open daily.

Helpful Contacts

St. Paul Area Chamber of Commerce

401 North Robert Street, Suite 150

St. Paul, MN 55101

651-223-5000

info@saintpaulchamber.com

www.saintpaulchamber.com

Science Museum of Minnesota

120 West Kellogg Boulevard

St. Paul, MN 55102

651-221-9444

Info@smm.org

www.smm.org

Hours: Open daily; call for hours and Omnitheater reservations.

(9) MOUNDS SPRINGS PARK, MINNESOTA VALLEY NATIONAL WILDLIFE REFUGE

Bloomington, MN

The Minnesota Valley National Wildlife Refuge (MVNWR) state recreation area stretches 34 miles from Fort Snelling west up the Minnesota River to Jordan and encompasses much of the traditional homelands of the Dakota peoples who settled this region, fishing and hunting and harvesting wild rice from the floodplain lakes. In places the river valley is 5 miles wide and 300 feet deep. The entire river valley was once crowded on both shores with clan villages and burial mound sites, but in modern times only a small remnant of these mound sites remains.

Most of the mound sites are carefully shielded from public access, but Mounds Springs Park, with twenty of its original thirty-six burial mounds in 125 undeveloped acres of terraces above the north bank river bottomlands, can be accessed from the MVNWR trail system or from the city streets of Bloomington on the bluffs above. The park is on the edge of a sizable residential district, and street parking is available. Bloomington is one of the Twin Cities metropolitan area's largest cities, with the International Airport and the Mall of America about fifteen minutes drive east from the park.

The entirety of the MVNWR, a major bird and wildlife migration point for the Upper Midwest, is traversed by hiking and bike paths through wetland, prairie, floodplain forest, and native grassland tracts, with frequent access points at carefully managed points along the river valley. Year-round recreational activities are available. The MVNWR's popular Wildlife Interpretation and Education Center—with a 125-seat auditorium, bookshop, observation deck, and 8,000 square feet of interpretive program and exhibit space on the river valley and its natural history—is just south of the airport on the river bluffs.

Mounds Springs Park

10201 11th Avenue South

Bloomington, MN 55420

952-948-8877 (Bloomington Parks and Recreation)

Directions: Take Highway 77 south to the exit at East Old Shakopee Road, and go west to Portland Avenue; or take I-35W south to the exit at East Old Shakopee Road, and go east to Portland Avenue. Take Portland south to 106th Street, go east to 10th Avenue, and go one-half block north—watch for the park entrance sign.

Helpful Contacts

City of Bloomington Convention and Visitors Bureau

7900 International Drive, Suite 990

Bloomington, MN 55425

cvb@bloomingtonmn.org

www.bloomingtonmn.org/attractions.asp

Minnesota Valley National Wildlife Refuge

Wildlife Interpretation and Education Center

3815 East 80th Street

Bloomington, MN 55425

612-854-5900

midwest.fws.gov/MinnesotaValley

(10) HISTORIC MURPHY'S LANDING, MINNESOTA VALLEY NATIONAL WILDLIFE REFUGE

Near Shakopee, MN

Historic Murphy's Landing, a popular living history county park on the south bank of the Minnesota River, is built around forty historic buildings moved to the site from around the region. The park, which presents life as it was at the time of statehood and the Civil War, also shelters sixteen burial mounds on its parklands that are estimated to be two thousand years old. It is reputed to be the site of the last war between the Ojibwe and the Dakota, and settlers are said to have watched the battle from the high bluffs above.

Historic Murphy's Landing (Three Rivers Park District)

2187 East Highway 101

Shakopee, MN 55379

952-445-6901

hmlstaff@threeriversparkdistrict.org

www.hennepinparks.org/outdoor_ed/murphys_landing/
   index.cfm

Directions: Take Highway 169 south to 101, and go west 4 miles to Murphy's Landing park entrance.

Hours: Open on weekends from May through October.

Admission: There is an admissions fee.

(11) MEMORIAL PARK

Shakopee, MN

The present-day city of Shakopee was established at the traditional village site of Dakota Chief Shakopee's people on the Minnesota River. The name comes from Teenataho-tonwa ("village of the prairie"), which was a community of summer bark lodges, winter tipis, and cornfields on the river terraces. The Shakopee Mdewakanton Sioux (Dakota) Community is just south of Shakopee at Prior Lake.

Shakopee's Memorial Park holds some of the few remaining burial mounds in the district. The mounds are fenced and can be easily approached for viewing. One of the Minnesota Valley National Wildlife Refuge trails is accessible from the park, which is just to the west of Murphy's Landing on the south bank of the Minnesota River.

Memorial Park (City of Shakopee)

East Highway 101

Shakopee, MN 55379

952-233-3800

Directions: Take Highway 169 south to 101, and go west 4 miles (past Murphy's Landing).

Helpful Contacts

Shakopee Mdewakanton Sioux (Dakota) Community

2330 Sioux Trail N.W.

Prior Lake, MN 55372

952-445-8900

www.ccsmdc.org

(12) BIRKMOSE PARK

Hudson, MN

Ancient burial mounds line the western side of Birkmose Park high on the St. Croix River bluffs in Hudson, Wisconsin, the gateway to Wisconsin from Minnesota. The mounds were noted in historic times as early as 1840 when a French Canadian built a small trading post nearby.

Modest interpretive signage can be found in the park; however, no barriers stand between the visitor and the mounds, and the mounds show evidence of considerable wear. Here great care should be taken to shepherd young visitors while observing the mounds.

Picnic grounds and pleasant walks are available. Views from the park are breathtaking, with full views north and south over the river.

Birkmose Park, City of Hudson

Coulee Road above Highway 35

Hudson, WI 54016

715-386-4765

info@ci.hudson.wi.us

www.ci.hudson.wi.us

Directions: One hour from the Twin Cities: I-94 over the St. Croix, take first exit to Highway 35, north on 35 one block to Coulee Road, turn right on Coulee Road to park entrance.

Hours: Open daily.

Helpful Contacts

Hudson Area Chamber of Commerce and Tourism

502 Second Street

Hudson, WI 54016

715-386-8411 or 800-657-6775

info@hudsonwi.org

www.hudsonwi.org

St. Croix Riverway

info@saintcroixriver.com

www.saintcroixriver.com/index.html

REGIONAL DAY TRIPS

Day trips from the Twin Cities metro area are fun and easy, taking the traveler down the Mississippi River to one of Minnesota's most delightful heritage tourism destinations or over the St. Croix River into Wisconsin's beautiful northwestern counties.

(13) RED WING ARCHAEOLOGICAL PRESERVE, CANNON VALLEY TRAIL

Red Wing, MN

The Cannon Valley Trail, stretching from the village of Cannon Falls to Red Wing on the Mississippi River, is one of the state's most popular rails-to-trails successes, converting the old track bedding of the Chicago Great Western Railroad to crushed limestone for long-distance bicycle touring recreation. The 19.7-mile trail parallels the Cannon River, creating one of the most sought-after recreational experiences in the greater metropolitan area.

The Cannon River has been a primary passage inland from the Mississippi River for thousands of years of habitation and trading. Vestiges of human occupation are everywhere in the valley, and extensive archaeological research has, to the present day, continued to explore the story of prehistoric settlement and culture.

The Institute for Minnesota Archaeology (IMA) is the primary research agency working in the Cannon River district and has, in cooperation with the city of Red Wing and the Goodhue County Historical Society, created an archaeology information station along the Cannon Valley Trail just below the Red Wing Archaeological Preserve, a district set aside for preservation and study. Volunteers from the IMA are available on the trail one day every month from May through September for "Voices of the Valley" programs to talk with visitors about the archaeology, geology, and natural history of the area.

A one-eighth-mile hiking path up to the reserve can be accessed from the trail (please note that accessibility is limited). Access to the trail is available at many points: information on accessing the trail at Red Wing is given below. Contact the IMA or the Goodhue County Historical Society for program information. Much of the historic city of Red Wing is a National Register District: do make plans to visit this most beautiful river city.

Red Wing Archaeological Preserve

Red Wing, MN 55066

Directions: *One hour from the Twin Cities:* Go south on U.S. 52 to State Highway 55, go east to Hastings, and then go south on U.S. 61 to Red Wing.

Trail access: *Lower A. P. Anderson Park Access:* Take the first right after the recycling center. There are signs posted on the highway to direct.

Helpful Contacts

Cannon Valley Trail
City Hall
306 West Mill Street
Cannon Falls, MN 55009
507-263-0508
info@cannonvalleytrail.com
www.cannonvalleytrail.com

Red Wing Visitor and Convention Bureau
418 Levee Street
Red Wing, MN 55066
651-385-5934 or 800-496-3444
www.redwing.org

Institute for Minnesota Archaeology
750 Transfer Road
St. Paul, MN 55114

651-848-0095

www.imnarch.org

Goodhue County Historical Society

1166 Oak Street

Red Wing, MN 55066

651-388-6024

goodhuecountyhis@qwest.net

www.goodhuehistory.mus.mn.us

(14) BIRD (OR BOW AND ARROW) PETROFORM

Near Hager City, WI

One of Wisconsin's few petroforms, this construction—a bird effigy or perhaps a bow and arrow—lies across the Mississippi River from Red Wing high on the bluff side above State Highway 35 at Hager City. Jacob Brower noted this petroform in 1902 while surveying the upper reaches of the Mississippi River and interpreted it as a bow and arrow pointing toward Lake Pepin, the great widening in the Mississippi River just downstream. Modern interpretation leans toward a bird effigy. Though the petroform has been there a considerable time, perhaps even since ancient times, no local tribal lore includes the story of this site.

This petroform was thought as late as the 1970s to be the only existing boulder effigy in Wisconsin; however, recent extensive research by the Mid-America Geological Society has revealed a great number of existing petroforms in the central and east-central region of the state.

Bird (or Bow and Arrow) Petroform

State Highway 35

Hager City, WI 54014

Directions: *From Red Wing:* Cross the Mississippi River on Highway 63 to Wisconsin, and go 1 mile south on Highway 35.

(15) INDIAN BURIAL GROUND

Near Spooner, WI

Spooner, Wisconsin, is one of many villages in this area of northwestern Wisconsin that developed along ancient Native American trade routes that later were adapted for use by European settlers, the railroad, and the timber industry. An ancient burial ground lies just west of Spooner on a widening in the Yellow River named Rice Lake, for the historic ricing beds that were found there. The gathering of mounds includes a rare Turtle "house" burial mound. In recent years bones that had been disinterred many years ago for research by a national university were reburied in a special ceremony with tribal members in attendance. Spooner is a popular recreation area and summer cabin destination for Twin Citians.

Indian Burial Ground

Spooner, WI 54801

Directions: *Two and a half hours from the Twin Cities: The slow scenic route:* Take I-94 to the St. Croix River, exit at Highway 95, go north through Stillwater to Taylors Falls, go east on U.S. 8 over the river through Turtle Lake, and go north on U.S. 63 to Spooner. *The faster route:* Take I-94 over the St. Croix River to Baldwin, and go north on U.S. 63 to Spooner. From Spooner go west on Highway 70 into Burnett County, turn right on County Road H and head north, cross the Yellow River, and take the first right turn, a circle road. The burial mounds overlook a historic wild rice field on Rice Lake, a widening in the Yellow River.

Helpful Contacts

Spooner Area Chamber of Commerce
122 North River Street
Spooner, WI 54801
715-635-2168
chamber@spooneronline.com
chamber.spooneronline.com, click on "City Government"

(16) INDIAN MOUNDS PARK
Rice Lake, WI

This park in the city of Rice Lake, Wisconsin, holds twelve of the original sixty-seven conical burial mounds that were built sometime after 500 C.E. Many of the mounds, which once covered a quarter mile of the lakeshore, were leveled through extensive excavations in recent centuries, including a study by the Smithsonian Institution. Other mounds were destroyed for city expansion and road building.

The Red Cedar River was dammed by a logging company to create Rice Lake: it was named for the many wild rice beds along the river. The Bayfield Trail, a traditional trading route for wild rice and pipestone, ran nearby; look for the historical marker noting the ancient rice beds and the ricing storage pits in the park.

Indian Mounds Park
Lakeshore Drive
Rice Lake, WI 54868
Directions: *Two and a half hours from the Twin Cities: The slow scenic*

route: Take I-94 to the St. Croix River, exit on Highway 95, go north through Stillwater to Taylors Falls, go east on U.S. 8 over the river through Turtle Lake and Barron, and go north on County Road SS to Rice Lake. *The faster route:* Take I-94 over the St. Croix River to Baldwin, go north on U.S. 63 to Turtle Lake, go east on U.S. 8 through Barron, and go north on County Road SS to Rice Lake.

Helpful Contacts

Rice Lake Chamber of Commerce
37 South Main Street
Rice Lake, WI 54868
715-234-2126

(17) WAKANDA PARK

Menomonie, WI

Three large oval mounds, known as the Upper Wakanda Mound Group, can be found in traditional placement on the terrace ridge above Lake Menomin, a widening in the Red Cedar River that forms the heart of this small city. An additional seventeen mounds were once located below this ridge, but 1950s dam construction flooded them out. Excavation prior to flooding indicated a radiocarbon date to sometime between 1000 and 1400 c.e. The headquarters of the Dunn County Historical Society is located in the park.

Wakanda Park

Pine Street at Lake Menomin
Menomonie, WI 54751
Directions: *Two and a half hours from the Twin Cities:* Take I-94

straight through to Menomonie, take the first Menomonie exit (#41), take a right at the stoplight, drive two blocks, take a left at the stoplight (a Super 8 is on the corner), turn left onto Pine, and drive to the park.

Helpful Contacts

Greater Menomonie Area Chamber of Commerce
700 Wolske Bay Road, Suite 200
Menomonie, WI 54751
800-283-1862
tourism@menomonie.org
www.menomonie.org

Russell J. Rassbach Heritage Museum
820 Wakanda Street
Menomonie, WI 54751
715-232-8685

CHAPTER 6

Minnesota's
Southwest Plains

In the southwestern part of the state, we leave behind the
majestic pine forests and the districts of deep hills and
river valleys. The southwestern plains of Minnesota are
the prairie lands of the state, flat tablelands moving toward
the Dakotas, the ancient shoreline of massive Glacial Lake
Aggasiz, and the vast drainage valley of Glacial River War-
ren. The farmlands stretch on seemingly forever, but there
are some hidden archaeological jewels amid the waving
grainfields and the prairie: two of Minnesota's premier
prehistoric sites.

(18) JEFFERS PETROGLYPHS
Near Comfrey, MN

The largest concentration of aboriginal rock art in the Upper Midwest can be found on a flat 300-yard-long bed of
exposed red quartzite on 80 acres in the fields above the
Little Cottonwood River in northern Cottonwood County.

Set at a low angle facing southwest, over two thousand carvings catch the varying light of the day and shine or fade as the sun passes from east to west. The range of petroglyph symbols found here is vast and universal: human figures, bows, arrows, darts and atlatls, buffalo, turtles, elk and deer, thunderbirds, sun figures, and shamans. The carvings were made by varying groups over a long period of time, some as early as 3,000 B.C.E. and some as late as 900 through 1700 C.E.

The Dakota people have served as stewards of the Jeffers Petroglyphs and partners in the preservation and interpretation of this magnificent cultural site. The Minnesota Historical Society has shepherded the site since 1966 and has recently built a handsome new interpretive building at the edge of the site. Self-guided tours are available on careful pathways through and around the carvings, and the virgin tallgrass prairie fields beyond the stone shelf are filled with wildflowers.

Jeffers Petroglyphs Historic Site

27160 County Road 2

Comfrey, MN 56019

507-628-5591

Jefferspetroglyphs@mnhs.com

Directions: *From Sioux Falls or Albert Lea:* Take I-90 east from Sioux Falls, SD, or west from Albert Lea, MN, to U.S. Highway 71 north through Jackson and Windom to County Road 10, go left to County Road 2, and go one mile south on 2. *Four hours from the Twin Cities:* Take Highway 169 south to Mankato, to Highway 60 into Windom; then go as above.

Hours: Open daily from Memorial Day through Labor Day and on weekends in May and September.

Admission: There is a small admission fee.

Helpful Contacts

Windom Area Chamber of Commerce
P.O. Box 8
Windom, MN 56101
507-831-2752
wacc@winwacc.com
www.winwacc.com

(19) PIPESTONE NATIONAL MONUMENT
Pipestone, MN

Pipestone, or catlinite, is quarried in an opening in the floor of the western plains of Minnesota at the edge of the tallgrass prairie sea that once covered the Dakotas. Much prized for pipe making, this soft, easily carved red stone was traded to both coasts and up and down the length of the Mississippi River. Quarrying at the Pipestone site has been a tradition of the Plains peoples for countless thousands of years: ceremonial smoking was essential to the Plains people, and pipes were stored as sacred objects. Ornamented and carved pipes were often buried with the dead.

The pipestone quarries remain in the stewardship of Dakota tribes of this region that have sole quarrying rights and continue to mine the beautiful red stone by traditional methods for traditional uses. So valuable was the Pipestone site considered to North American history that the site was designated a National Monument by the U.S. government in 1937.

Although the quarries themselves, described by a European explorer as "two miles in length and thirty feet high" are closed to the public, much of the general site is open for interpreted tours (summer) and self-tours on the Circle Trail past native prairie and the beautiful cascade named Winnewissa Falls. Exceptional petroglyph imagery remains on rock slabs broken off of larger rock walls by European explorers; fortunately the rock art has been rescued and is on display in the Visitor Center for study. The Visitor Center and the Upper Midwest Indian Cultural Center are the welcome point for visitors and are wheelchair accessible.

Pipestone National Monument

36 Reservation Avenue

Pipestone, MN 56164-1269

507-825-5464

www.nps.gov/pipe/index.htm

Directions: *From the south:* Take I-90 east from Sioux Falls, SD, or west from Albert Lea, MN, to U.S. Highway 75 north through Luverne through Pipestone, and watch for signs to the park.

Five hours from the Twin Cities: Take Highway 169 south to Mankato, to Highway 14 west to Lake Benson, go south on U.S. Highway 75 to Pipestone, and watch for signs to the park.

Hours: Open daily except Christmas Day and New Year's Day.

Admission: There is a small admission fee.

CHAPTER 7

The Driftless Area

The "Driftless Area," the Upper Midwest's vast unglaciated district, is a topography of high cliffs and deep, cold, fast-rushing streams, all moving toward the Mississippi River from points in southeastern Minnesota, northeastern Iowa, and southwestern Wisconsin. Here the topography cares nothing for the political boundaries of the state lines. Using bridges and byways and the Great River Road we can cross this unique landscape and admire the remnants of past peoples, who left clan symbols and ceremonial imagery in the form of effigy mounds and petroglyphs, and honor the quiet upland meadows with their sleeping burial mounds.

To try and separate sites on opposite sides of the river would be to dishonor the intentions of the past peoples, who placed their effigies, campsites, and heavenly observation posts atop the great cliffs above the river, often in sight of the other shore. So complete a district is this region that you are encouraged to explore these parks as much as your time permits. Bridges over the Mississippi include:

- La Crescent, Minnesota, to La Crosse, Wisconsin (two bridges);
- Lansing, Iowa, to De Soto/Ferryville, Wisconsin, via the Blackhawk Bridge;
- Marquette, Iowa, to Prairie du Chien, Wisconsin; and
- Millville/Turkey River, Iowa, to Cassville, Wisconsin, via the Cassville Car Ferry.

(20) PERROT STATE PARK

Near Trempealeau, WI

Beautiful Perrot is one of the jewels of the Wisconsin park system, not just for its vast natural wonders and myriad recreational opportunities but also because so much remains of the ways in which Wisconsin's earliest peoples once lived, worked, and worshiped. It is true that much has been destroyed of those cultural remnants—some unfortunate stories indeed: effigy and conical burial mounds leveled, rock art sites dismantled so that the stone could be used for road building and bridge supports. To the rescue have come two factors: (1) the painstaking draftsmanship of the early surveyors who documented the mounds and the petroglyphs and (2) the belief of the state of Wisconsin that these cultural inheritances must be shepherded and, where possible, reinterpreted for the public.

A unique partnership among the State Historical Society of Wisconsin, the Ho-Chunk (Winnebago) Nation, and the Mississippi Valley Archaeology Center of the University of Wisconsin–La Crosse has enabled the building of an exhibit hall with interpretive displays, the re-creation of petroglyph panels, and the careful stewardship of the remaining mounds. Many of the remaining sites are easily viewed, and public programming is available during the summer months for visitors. The 1,400 acres of the park offer 500-foot-high bluff views over the confluence of the Trempealeau and Mississippi Rivers. Visitors can hike to the goat prairies of the Brady Bluff State Natural Area, look for birds and animals at the Trempealeau National Wildlife Refuge, take bicycles down the Great River Trail, or hike to the top of the 425-foot-high Trempealeau Mountain, still considered sacred ground by the Ho-Chunk and graced with beautiful effigy mounds.

Perrot State Park

W26247 Sullivan Road, P.O. Box 407
Trempealeau, WI 54661-0407
608-534-6409
Directions: *One hour from La Crosse:* Go north on State Highway 35 (Great River Road) through the village of Trempealeau to the park.
Hours: Open daily.
Admission: There is a state parks admission fee.

Helpful Contacts

Historic Trempealeau Village
Trempealeau Chamber of Commerce
P.O. Box 212
Trempealeau, WI 54661
608-534-6780
chamber@trempealeau.net
www.trempealeau.net/village_intro.htm

Mississippi Valley Archaeology Center
University of Wisconsin–La Crosse

1725 State Street
La Crosse, WI 54601
608-785-8463
www.uwlax.edu/mvac

(21) MYRICK PARK

La Crosse, WI

Myrick Park shelters small effigy and conical burial mounds, once excavated in the 1880s by members of Harvard's Peabody Museum, in a large parkland that includes the city zoo, picnic areas, and recreation opportunities. The adjacent La Crosse River Marsh Trail system has hiking and nature trails.

Myrick Park

2100 La Crosse Street
La Crosse, WI 54601
608-789-7533 (La Crosse Parks and Recreation)
Directions: *From I-90:* Take the U.S. 53 (Rose Street) exit south through the city, and go left on La Crosse Street past the university campus to the park. *From La Crescent:* Take Highway 14/61 over the river into La Crosse to 12th Street North, go left on 12th Street to La Crosse Street, and turn left past the university campus to the park.

Helpful Contacts

La Crosse Area Convention and Visitor's Bureau
410 East Veteran's Memorial Drive
La Crosse, WI 54601
608-782-2366 or 800-658-9424
info@explorelacrosse.com
www.explorelacrosse.com/home/index.asp

(22) RIVERSIDE CEMETERY

Near Genoa, WI

Among its historic graves and headstones, the pastoral Riverside Cemetery, high above the Mississippi River on the Great River Road, shelters nine of the remaining ancient conical burial mounds among the many once mapped by Increase Lapham in 1852.

Riverside Cemetery

Great River Road

Genoa, WI 54632

Helpful Contacts

Hometown Genoa

www.rhometown.com/WI/Genoa

Walworth County Historical Society

9 East Rockwell, P.O. Box 273

Elkhorn, WI 53121

262-723-4248

walcohistory@elknet.net

www.geocities.com/walcohistory

Hours: Open afternoons Wednesday–Saturday or by appointment in late May through mid-October (call for hours).

(23) FISH FARM MOUNDS STATE PRESERVE

Near New Albin, IA

There are few sights more stirring than that seen the moment one climbs the steep shelving steps up to this small meadow opening among the trees to see the twenty-eight tall, conical, grass-covered burial mounds, all in close groups and somehow always in a soft light that seems to be part of this landscape. Fish Farm Mounds was originally surveyed by Daniel Boone's son, Captain Nathan Boone, in 1832. The Woodland mounds, dated at 200 B.C.E. to 400 C.E., on the 500-acre preserve are typical of the many mounds that once dotted the bluff tops along the river but have long since been destroyed.

The park is now maintained as an Iowa State Preserve, and the Ho-Chunk and Iowa Nations have shared stewardship of the cemetery. A wayside rest is available below by the small parking lot.

Fish Farm Mounds State Preserve

Highway 26

New Albin, IA 52160

Directions: Go 3 miles south from New Albin or 6 miles north from Lansing on the Great River Road to the wayside rest area (Highway 26, just over the state line).

(24) SLINDE MOUNDS STATE PRESERVE

Near Hanover, IA

The Slinde Mounds are found in the traditional mounds site on a terrace high above the Upper Iowa River. There are sixteen conical burial mounds of the Woodland era here sheltered in a 32-acre state preserve that is open to nonmotorized activities and seasonal hunting.

There are no park facilities on the preserve. A small parking bay is available at the preserve entrance.

Directions: *From the River Road at Lansing:* Take Highway 9 west to Waukon. From Waukon take County A52 west 2 miles to County W60. Turn north on County W60 and travel about 6 winding miles. Bear left (west) where County W60 turns north. Go about one mile north and west, and then turn north before crossing the Upper Iowa River. Go north for about 1.5 miles, crossing the river, to the preserve on the north side of the road. (It's complicated . . . but very worth it!)

(25) EFFIGY MOUNDS NATIONAL MONUMENT
Near Marquette, IA

Considered the premier archaeological site of the Upper Midwest, the Effigy Mounds National Monument commands a great sweep of the Mississippi River Valley. It is the first of three major prehistoric bluffland sites that overlook the massive confluence delta of the Wisconsin and Mississippi Rivers at Prairie du Chien (see also Pike's Peak State Park and Wyalusing State Park).

Long shepherded by the National Park Service and held in stewardship by the Iowa Nation, this magnificent tract of river uplands is graced with 31 enormous effigy mounds, 164 conical burial mounds, and over 2,500 acres of woodland overlooking the river meadows from great heights. Eleven miles of hiking trails wander through bluffland, forest, wetlands, and open tallgrass prairie.

The effigy mounds that give this great parkland its name represent mammals, birds, reptiles, and linear shapes, but the most famous of the effigy symbols is the bear, seen in many places in the park. The Great Bear Mound is 137 feet long and 3.5 feet high. Most popular are the wonderful Marching Bears that spread in a line across an open hillside high above the bluffs. The mounds are of Woodland origin, with estimated dates ranging from 500 B.C.E. to 1300 C.E.

There is an excellent Visitors Center at the park entrance, done in the customary quality style of the National Park Service, with excellent interpretive exhibits and educational programs. A first-rate bookshop can also be found here.

There are no camping or lodging facilities in the park, but there are many options in nearby Harpers Ferry, Marquette, and McGregor and across the river in Prairie du Chien. There are no roads in the park above the Visitors Center and, unfortunately, no accessible sites except for three mounds down on the lowest level of the park. Note to hikers: The preliminary walking path up to the bluffs is quite steep and somewhat long.

Effigy Mounds National Monument

151 Highway 76

Harpers Ferry, IA 52146-7519

563-873-349

www.nps.gov/efmo

Directions: Go 3 miles north of Marquette on Highway 76 (or 6 miles across the Mississippi River from Prairie du Chien, WI).

Hours: Open daily except Thanksgiving, Christmas Day, and New Year's Day.

Helpful Contacts

McGregor–Marquette Chamber of Commerce

146 Main Street, Box 105

McGregor, IA 52157

563-873-2186 or 800-896-0910

mac-marq@alpinecom.net

www.mcgreg-marq.org

Prairie du Chien Area Chamber of Commerce

800-732-1673

info@prairieduchien.org

www.prairieduchien.org

(26) PIKE'S PEAK STATE PARK

Near McGregor, IA

Named for Zebulon Pike's visit here in 1805, Pike's Peak State Park is the second of three major prehistoric bluffland sites that overlook the massive confluence delta of the Wisconsin and Mississippi Rivers at Prairie du Chien (see also Effigy Mounds National Monument and Wyalusing State Park). Pike's Peak comprises nearly 1,000 acres of wooded valleys and rolling hills, with 13 miles of hiking trails and camping sites. The great Decorah limestone bluffs filled with fossils and the lovely Bridal Veil Falls are well worth seeing. The park shelters, among its many year-round recreational amenities, several mounds including a very fine Bear effigy mound high on an overlook above the river, a mirror image to that found just upriver at Effigy Mounds National Monument. Many of the facilities and picnic overlook sites in the park are fully accessible, as is the Bear effigy mound.

Pike's Peak State Park

15316 Great River Road

McGregor, IA 52157-8558

563-873-2341

Pikes_Peak@dnearstate.ia.us

www.state.ia.us/dnr/organiza/ppd/pikepeak.htm

Directions: *From McGregor (or Prairie du Chien through Marquette):*
Follow Highway 340 south out of McGregor 1.5 miles to the
park entrance.

Hours: Open daily.

Admission: There are camping fees.

Helpful Contacts

McGregor–Marquette Chamber of Commerce
146 Main Street, Box 105
McGregor, IA 52157
563-873-2186 or 800-896-0910
mac-marq@alpinecom.net
www.mcgreg-marq.org

Prairie du Chien Area Chamber of Commerce
800-732-1673
info@prairieduchien.org
www.prairieduchien.org

(27) WYALUSING STATE PARK

Near Prairie du Chien, WI

Downriver only a short way from Effigy Mounds National
Monument and Pike's Peak State Park, Wyalusing State
Park is the third of the three major prehistoric bluffland
sites that overlook the massive confluence delta of the
Wisconsin and Mississippi Rivers at Prairie du Chien. The
magnificent siting high on the bluffs above the river delta
makes this one of Wisconsin's most majestic forested parklands. There are prairie uplands, sand caves, waterfalls,
and intriguing rock formations to be seen in its 2,600
acres. The area was certainly attractive to many of the re-

gion's native peoples, with its beauty and its strategic location. As many as 130 mounds once were found here on Sentinel Ridge, drawing researchers from the Bureau of Ethnology of the Smithsonian Institution in the 1880s. Over half of the mounds were eventually destroyed by farming or stone quarrying, but the remaining sixty-nine bear, water spirit, and compound effigy and conical burial mounds are revered by the Ho-Chunk and Iowa Nations, who are the present-day stewards of these ancient sites.

Wyalusing has established a beautifully designed natural history interpretive center and has placed many historical markers throughout for visitors interested in the history and prehistory of the park. Twenty-two miles of hiking are available as well as several miles of interpretive nature trails and extensive, groomed mountain bike paths. A unique canoe trail through the river bottoms permits the visitor to see the diverse plant and animal life of the water meadows.

Wyalusing State Park

13081 State Park Lane

Bagley, WI 53801

608-996-2261

www.dnearstate.wi.us/org/land/parks/specific/wyalusing

Directions: *From Prairie du Chien:* Take U.S. 18/State Highway 35 south through Bridgeport, cross the Wisconsin River to County Road C, turn right heading west on C to County Road X, turn right on X, and go one mile to the park entrance.

Hours: Open daily.

Admission: There are admission and camping fees.

Helpful Contacts

Friends of Wyalusing
www.wyalusing.org

McGregor–Marquette Chamber of Commerce
146 Main Street, Box 105
McGregor, IA 52157
563-873-2186 or 800-896-0910
mac-marq@alpinecom.net
www.mcgreg-marq.org

Prairie du Chien Area Chamber of Commerce
800-732-1673
info@prairieduchien.org
www.prairieduchien.org

(28) NELSON DEWEY STATE PARK
Near Cassville, WI

Nelson Dewey State Park, named for the state's first governor, is one of Wisconsin's smaller state parks, but its features include 20 acres of native prairie (designated a State Natural Area), miles of hiking trails, a self-guided nature trail, bluff-top camping sites, and a historic village site overlooking the 100,000-acre tract of the Upper Mississippi River Wildlife and Fish Refuge. The park also shelters conical, linear, and effigy mounds, easily accessible and visible from the Mound Point Trail, with benches along the way to allow relaxed viewing of wildlife and birds on the flyway above the river. Historic Cassville is just south of the park, and the river can be crossed there on the Cassville Car Ferry from May through October.

Nelson Dewey State Park

County Road VV, Box 658

Cassville, WI 53806

608-725-5374

Directions: *From Cassville:* Go north 2 miles on County Road VV
(Great River Road) to the park entrance.

Hours: Open daily (may occasionally be closed because of snow;
call for conditions update).

Admission: There are admission and camping fees.

Helpful Contacts

Cassville Tourism

P.O. Box 576

Cassville, WI 53806

608-725-5855

casstour@pcii.net

www.cassville.org

Cassville Car Ferry

Between Cassville, Wisconsin, and Millville (Turkey River),
    Iowa

608-725-5180 (local information and crossing conditions)

Hours: Open weekends in May until Memorial Day; open daily
until Labor Day; open weekends to October 31.

(29) TURKEY RIVER MOUNDS STATE PRESERVE

Near Turkey River and Millville, IA

This 62-acre state preserve shelters an unusual range of
geological, archaeological, and biological resources within
one tract at the meeting of the Turkey River and the Mississippi. Numerous prairies and woodlands can be studied
here.

The preserve's exceptional feature is a Galena dolomite ridge that rises 250 feet above the river valley; it is some 1,000 feet wide at one end and yet only a few feet wide at the other. The view over the Mississippi is spectacular.

In company on the ridge top are forty-three burial mounds surrounded by a semicircular ditch built by Late Woodland people between 500 B.C.E. and 900 C.E. Artifacts found in earlier excavation studies of the mounds indicate that trade was ranging as far away as the Gulf Coast. The mounds are now held in stewardship by the Iowa Nation.

As with many of the state's preserves, there are no facilities on site. Vehicles can be left at a small parking lot near the preserve; visitors hike in on a trail.

Directions: *From Guttenberg (on the Great River Road):* Take U.S. 52 south about 5.5 miles, take the last left turn before crossing the Turkey River, drive one mile on a gravel road that will bring you to a parking lot, and take the trail to the preserve. *From Cassville:* Take the Cassville Car Ferry to the west bank of the Mississippi; the road from the ferry landing will take you to a T intersection. Bear right until you get into Millville and U.S. 52, then take 52 over the Turkey River and take the first right turn onto a gravel road, go one mile to the parking lot on the north side of the road, and take the trail to the preserve.

Hours: Open daily (there is a low-maintenance gravel road; flooding or snow conditions may close the road).

Helpful Contacts

Historic Guttenberg
Guttenberg Civic and Commerce Club
323 South River Park Drive, P.O. Box 536
Guttenberg, IA 52052

563-252-2323 or 877-252-2323
gutnberg@alpinecom.net
www.alpinecom.net/~gutnberg

Cassville Tourism
P.O. Box 576
Cassville, WI 53806
608-725-5855
casstour@pcii.net
www.cassville.org

Cassville Car Ferry
Between Cassville, Wisconsin, and Millville (Turkey River),
     Iowa
608-725-5180 (local information and crossing conditions)
Hours: Open weekends in May until Memorial Day; open daily
until Labor Day; open weekends to October 31.

Dubuque and Points South

The Mississippi River continues to be the focal point for many of the archaeology parks of this region on both sides of the river. Here we leave Wisconsin and much of the effigy mound culture that we have become so familiar with in the upper reaches of the river in the Driftless Area. The middle Mississippi River district becomes a region of rolling hills and sandy shoals with broad hardwood stands on the upper hills. We will wander down the Iowa side of the river and back into some of the beautiful river valleys coming down in the hills west of the Mississippi; then we will make our way back to the Great River and finally cross into Illinois.

(30) LITTLE MAQUOKETA RIVER MOUNDS STATE PRESERVE
Near Dubuque, IA

The Little Maquoketa River Preserve, a recent addition to the Iowa State Preserve system, shelters thirty-two ancient burial mounds atop a 200-foot-long limestone ridge above the stream of the same name. The preserve holds 41 acres of hardwood forest and native prairie remnants, with a hiking trail up to the high bluff top and circling the mounds, which range from 13 to 42 feet across and between 6 and 50 feet in height. Built by the Woodland people, the mounds have been dated to between 700 and 1300 C.E. The mounds are protected by fencing and are interpreted with informational kiosks with detailed panels on the archaeological, geological, and biological resources of the site that can be found at the parking lot below and at the bluff top.

The Little Maquoketa River Mounds State Preserve was developed in consultation with fifteen area Native American tribal communities and is managed on behalf of the state of Iowa by the Dubuque County Conservation Board. Information on the preserve can be found by contacting the board's Swiss Valley Nature Center in Peosta.

Little Maquoketa River Mounds State Preserve

(Dubuque County Conservation Board, Peosta, IA)

U.S. 52/Highway 3

Dubuque, IA 52004

563-556-6745 (Swiss Valley Nature Center)

Directions: *From Dubuque:* Take U.S. 52 and Iowa 3 about 2 miles north from the city limits, and watch for the preserve marker and parking lot on the west side of the road.

Hours: Open daily from sunrise to sunset.

Helpful Contacts

Dubuque Area Chamber of Commerce

300 Main Street, Suite 200

P.O. Box 705

Dubuque, IA 52004-0705

563-557-9200

office@dubuquechamber.com

www.dubuquechamber.com

(31) CATFISH CREEK STATE PRESERVE, MINES OF SPAIN RECREATION AREA

Near Dubuque, IA

The 600-acre Catfish Creek Preserve is a tract within a larger park district on the west bank of the Mississippi River, taking its name from a now-entrenched stream that once flowed into the river before erosion of the bluffs closed off the stream course. Settlement in the Catfish Creek area can be dated back almost eight thousand years, with evidence of steady use of rock shelters, campsites, and villages. The preserve shelters groups of mounds and other burial sites.

It is thought that these ancient peoples may have opened the first lead mines, which were later named by Spanish explorers who traded with the Mesquakie Nation settled here in the late 1700s. Mines of Spain, as the district is now named, is designated a National Historic Landmark as well as a National Wildlife Federation Nature Area. The preserve offers upland prairies and tracts of lowland forest and wetlands.

Catfish Creek Preserve

Mines of Spain State Recreation Area

8999 Bellevue Heights

Dubuque, IA 52003

563-556-0620

Mines_of_Spain@dnearstate.ia.us

www.state.ia.us/dnr/organiza/ppd/minesof.htm

Directions: The Mines of Spain State Recreation Area is on the south edge of Dubuque. Access to the park is off U.S. 52 South, which intersects with U.S. 61/151 on the south side of the city. The Catfish Creek Preserve can be reached via the main park entrance road.

 Helpful Contacts

Dubuque Area Chamber of Commerce

300 Main Street, Suite 200

P.O. Box 705

Dubuque, IA 52004-0705

563-557-9200

office@dubuquechamber.com

www.dubuquechamber.com

(32) BELLEVUE STATE PARK

Bellevue, IA

This bluffland park above the Mississippi River is divided into two districts: the Nelson Unit on the north, offering hiking and picnic sites, and the Dyas Unit on the south, offering hiking and self-guided nature trails and campsites. The park also holds the South Bluff Nature Center, with its lovely "Garden Sanctuary for Butterflies."

Trail #2 in the Nelson Unit trails leads to three conical burial mounds high above the river. The mounds were built by the Woodland people and have been dated between 1,000 B.C.E. and 1300 C.E. Bellevue State Park is a popular bird-watching and wildflower visitor destination.

Bellevue State Park

21466 29th Avenue

Bellevue, WI 52031

563-872-4019

www.state.ia.us/dnr/organiza/ppd/bellevue.htm

Directions: *From Dubuque:* Go 21 miles south on U.S. 52.

Hours: Open daily.

Admission: There are camping fees.

Helpful Contacts

Bellevue Chamber of Commerce

563-872-5830

www.bellevueia.com

(33) WICKIUP HILL OUTDOOR LEARNING CENTER

Near Cedar Rapids, IA

This new environmental educational center opened in October 2002 to much acclaim for its innovative and attractive environmental education programs and teaching facility. Named for the type of temporary bark-and-brush frame dwelling used by nomadic Native Americans, the Wickiup Center was developed in cooperation with many state and tribal partners to provide exhibits and learning opportunities on Native American life and archaeological field study, as well as outdoor recreational and environmental learning.

The 10,000-square-foot Learning Center occupies a 240-acre site in the midst of a large 563-acre parcel of woodland, wetland, and prairie on the Cedar River Greenbelt just north of Cedar Rapids. It is operated in cooperation with the Linn County Conservation Board.

Wickiup Hill Outdoor Learning Center

10260 Morris Hills Road

Toddville, IA 52341

319-892-6485

cons.edu@linncounty.org

www.linncountyparks.com/index.asp

Directions: *From Cedar Rapids:* Go north on I-380 to the Boyson Road exit; go left on Boyson, left again on Miller/Buffalo Road, and right on Blairs Ferry Road; continue winding west and north on Blairs Ferry Road to Feather Ridge Road, turn right and drive north one mile, go left onto Morris Hills Road, and go west one mile to the park entrance.

Hours: Open on Wednesday through Sunday. Hours vary; call for hours and programs.

(34) INDIAN FISH TRAP STATE PRESERVE

Near Amana, IA

This preserve is named for the 200-foot-long prehistoric rock funnel used for fishing the ancient Iowa River from the nearby fortified Wittrock Village site, thought to be occupied circa 100 C.E. for several hundred years. Fish were driven into the trap funnel, or weir, at the upstream end and forced to the narrow end downstream where they were caught by hand to be held in an adjacent pool. It is thought that glacial boulders eroding from the riverbank were used to craft the trap. Experiments were conducted in the late 1980s by the Iowa Archaeological Society to determine how to use the rock funnel.

The site is on the National Register of Historic Places. No facilities are available at the preserve. The Amana Na-

Visitors traveling up the Rainy River by steamboat to view the Manitou Mounds on the Minnesota-Canada border, 1914. *(Courtesy of the Minnesota Historical Society)*

The Grand Mound near International Falls, Minnesota, c. 1915. *(Courtesy of the Minnesota Historical Society)*

Indian Mounds Park on Daytons Bluff overlooking the Mississippi River in St. Paul. Note that walking ramps have been carved out of the mounds themselves to permit easier climbing. Today's park site reflects considerable restoration of the mounds. *(Courtesy of the author)*

Carver's Cave, a legendary landmark just below Indian Mounds Park on the Mississippi at St. Paul's Daytons Bluff, was eventually blocked by railroad tracks and used for storage. It lost most of its rock art to vandalism years ago and has been sealed against further desecration. *(Courtesy of the Minnesota Historical Society)*

The entrance to the Birkmose Park burial mounds site high above the St. Croix at Hudson, Wisconsin, c. 1940. *(Courtesy of the author)*

Researchers excavating a mound site near Lake of the Isles in Minneapolis, Minnesota, c. 1910. Conical burial mounds were once found in great quantity west of Minneapolis around the district of Lake Minnetonka. As many as 90 percent of those mounds were destroyed by development. *(Courtesy of the author)*

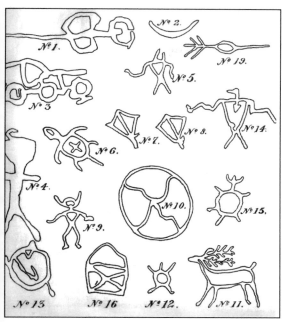

Detail, Thunderbird, Jeffers Petroglyphs drawings. *(Courtesy of Winchell and Lewis 1911)*

T. H. Lewis's drawings of the Jeffers Petroglyphs in southwestern Minnesota, c. 1880. *(Courtesy of Winchell and Lewis 1911)*

The Jeffers Thunderbird today ("chalked" lines created by digital enhancement). *(Courtesy of Charles R. Bailey)*

The petroglyphs panels from the Pipestone Quarries, 1902. These stunning carvings were once a part of the massive Three Maidens boulders near the quarries, but were broken off in the 1880s in a misguided attempt to protect the images. The slabs are now on display at the Pipestone Visitor Center. *(Courtesy of the Minnesota Historical Society)*

At the Pipestone Quarries, 1883. Present-day tribal communities have traditional quarrying rights to the pipestone. *(Courtesy of the Minnesota Historical Society)*

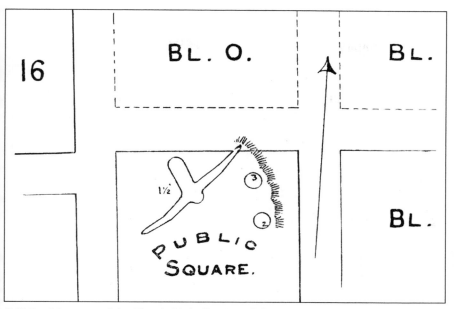

T. H. Lewis's survey of the Thunderbird effigy in Hokah, Minnesota, c. 1880. *(Courtesy of Winchell and Lewis 1911)*

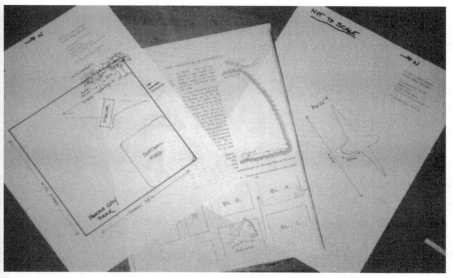

The author's re-survey of the Hokah Park Thunderbird (thought lost), 1994. *(Courtesy of the author)*

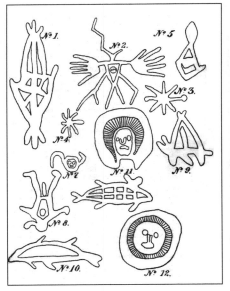

Chert seam grooves. These ancient concentric circle grooves were found by the author near quantities of worked stone along a chert seam high in the bluffs above the Mississippi River in southeastern Minnesota. Chert was the most popular stone used to make blades and points (arrowheads) for hunting and skinning. *(Courtesy of the author)*

Ancient petroglyphs at Minnesota's Reno Cave above the Mississippi River as recorded by T. H. Lewis, c. 1880. Today the carvings are virtually obliterated at this ancient site high in the blufflands in the Driftless Area. The drawings by early surveyors are often our only record of lost rock art and effigy mound sites. *(Courtesy of Winchell and Lewis 1911)*

The author and colleagues surveying for rock art on the river bluffs on the Upper Mississippi River, Minnesota, 1995. The distinctive vertical gouge marks on the sandstone are called "groovings." Teams of specialists in cultural resource management work to bring together archaeological, historical, and tribal perspectives on the Upper Midwest's vast cultural inheritance. *(Courtesy of Charles R. Bailey)*

The Fish Farm Mounds park site on the Mississippi River near New Albin, Iowa. One of the most dramatic burial mound sites in the state of Iowa, comprising several dozen high conical mounds in close proximity, Fish Farm Mounds is a favorite with photographers as they work to capture the light at different times of the day. *(Courtesy of Lori Stanley)*

An early map held by the Wisconsin Historical Society of a great effigy mound site in the Wisconsin Territory, 1838. *(Courtesy of the Wisconsin Historical Society)*

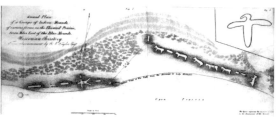

Wisconsin Territory, Detail, Marching Bears. *(Courtesy of the Wisconsin Historical Society)*

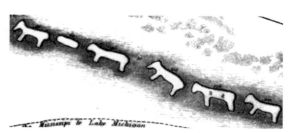

The famous Marching Bears of the Effigy Mounds National Monument as seen above the Mississippi River at McGregor, Iowa. *(Courtesy of R. Clark Mallam Collection/Lori Stanley)*

Three men left a detailed legacy of Upper Midwest effigy mounds, rock art and other prehistoric site maps surveyed in the nineteenth century that are used today to reclaim and restore these same archaeological sites:

Jacob Brower's research and explorations in Minnesota focused on the upper reaches of the Mississippi River in the late 1880s. *(Courtesy of the author)*

Theodore Hayes (T. H.) Lewis surveyed many of Minnesota's burial mound and rock art sites in the 1880s for the Northwestern Archaeological Survey. *(Courtesy of the author)*

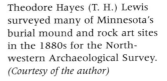

Increase Lapham, a naturalist and engineer, surveyed many of Wisconsin's ancient earthworks between 1835 and 1855. *(Courtesy of the author)*

Early drawings of the lost Trempeauleau petroglyphs on the Wisconsin side of the Mississippi River. These drawings enabled present-day archaeologists to re-create the carvings in an exhibit at Perrot State Park. *(Courtesy of Lapham 1855)*

The famous rock carvings at Roche-a-Cri in northern Wisconsin. The great column of rock is one of that state's most famous archaeological icons. *(Courtesy of Lapham 1855)*

The famous Panther Intaglio on the Rock River at Fort Atkinson, Wisconsin, c. 1910. This intaglio (from the Italian word for a grooved printing plate) is one of the few remaining such effigies in the Upper Midwest. *(Courtesy of the Wisconsin Historical Society)*

The Jefferson County Indian Mound and Trails Park at Wisconsin's Lake Koshkonong. This park is built around an ancient effigy mound district in south central Wisconsin. *(Courtesy of the author)*

The Mound Cemetery at Racine, Wisconsin, c. 1910. It was not uncommon to establish Upper Midwest historic cemeteries on the same site as prehistoric burial mounds, thus continuing a tradition of interring the dead on sanctified ground. *(Courtesy of the Wisconsin Historical Society)*

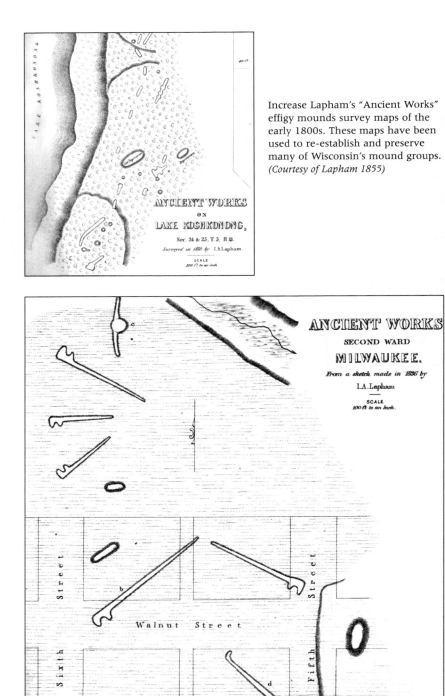

Increase Lapham's "Ancient Works" effigy mounds survey maps of the early 1800s. These maps have been used to re-establish and preserve many of Wisconsin's mound groups. *(Courtesy of Lapham 1855)*

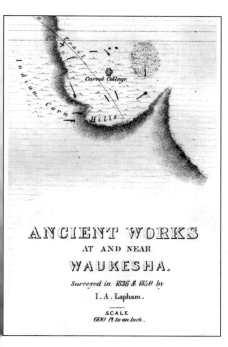

ANCIENT WORKS
AT AND NEAR
WAUKESHA.

Surveyed in 1836 & 1850 by
I. A. Lapham.

SCALE
600 ft. to an inch.

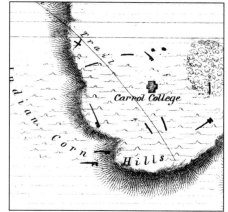

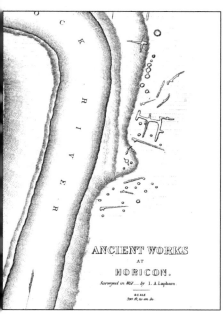

ANCIENT WORKS
AT
HORICON.

Surveyed in 1851 ..... by I. A. Lapham.

SCALE
200 ft. to an in.

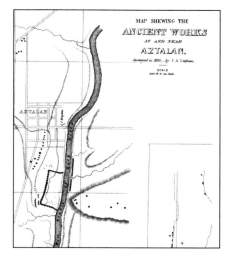

MAP SHEWING THE
ANCIENT WORKS
AT AND NEAR
AZTALAN.

Surveyed in 1850 .... by I. A. Lapham.

SCALE
2000 ft. to an Inch.

A turtle effigy mound revealed by melting
spring snow on the University of
Wisconsin Campus, c. 1950. *(Courtesy of the
Wisconsin Historical Society)*

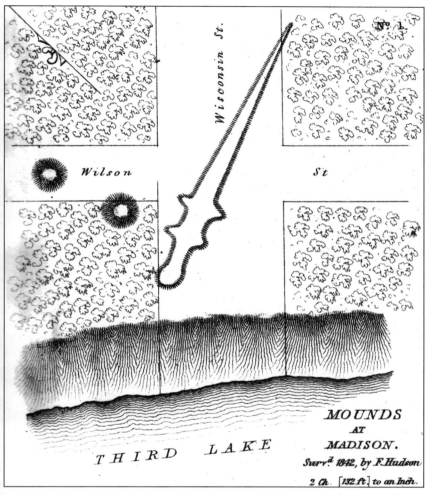

Increase Lapham's detail of
one of many of Madison's
effigy mounds, c. 1850.
(Courtesy of Lapham 1855)

A deer effigy on the grounds of the State
Hospital on the edges of the City of
Madison, 1919. Note the chalked outline of
the effigy mound that reveals the shape of
the earthwork. Today great care is taken
working with effigy mounds and also with
rock art: chalking, glazing, outlining, and
rubbings of any kind are now actively dis-
couraged in favor of modern photographic
and lighting technologies that permit accu-
rate dating of surfaces and sites. *(Courtesy of
the Wisconsin Historical Society)*

ture Trail leads two miles on foot into the preserve from the small parking area. The nearby Amana Colonies are a delightful heritage travel destination.

Directions: *From Cedar Rapids:* Follow U.S. 151 south through Amana to U.S. 6, and look for the Amana Nature Trail parking area about 50 yards just west of the intersection.

Hours: Open daily.

Helpful Contacts

Amana Colonies Convention and Visitors Bureau
39 38th Avenue, Suite 100
Amana, IA 52203
319-622-7622 or 800-579-2294
info@amanacolonies.com
www.amanacolonies.com

(35) TOOLESBORO MOUNDS STATE PRESERVE
Toolesboro, IA

The seven Toolesboro Mounds, a National Historic Landmark, are sheltered in one of Iowa's earliest state preserves on a bluff overlooking the delta of the Iowa River where it flows into the Mississippi. Dated from 100 B.C.E. to 200 C.E., the mounds are known to be of Hopewell (Middle Woodland) construction and once numbered a dozen. The largest of the mounds, Mound 2, measures 100 feet in diameter and 8 feet in height and is thought to be the largest Hopewell mound in the state. The Hopewell people were known to travel and trade extensively, employing tools and crafted items from both coasts, the Great Lakes, and the Gulf of Mexico. The burial mounds at Toolesboro are unique in that they have inner wooden chambers for the dead.

There is an interpretive center with exhibits on the grounds and a demonstration prairie plot that re-creates what the Hopewell people would have found when they lived here. The site is in the stewardship of the State Historical Society of Iowa, in partnership with regional tribal communities, and is managed for the society by the Louisa County Conservation Board.

Toolesboro Mounds State Preserve

Highway 99

Toolesboro, IA 52653

Directions: *From Muscatine:* Travel south on U.S. 61/Highway 92 approximately 20 miles to Wapello and then 8 miles east on Iowa 99 to Toolesboro. The preserve is one block north of the highway on the west side of town.

Hours: Open afternoons daily from late May through Labor Day; open on weekend afternoons from Labor Day through October 31—or by appointment.

Admission: Free.

Helpful Contacts

Louisa County Conservation Board

Box 261

Wapello, IA 52653

319-523-8381

Muscatine Convention and Visitors Bureau

319 East Second Street, Suite 102

Muscatine, IA 52761

563-263-8895 or 800-257-3275

www.meetmuscatine.com

(36) JAMES WEED PARK

Muscatine, IA

Weed Park, one of Muscatine's largest and loveliest city parklands, occupies an enviable spot on a heavily forested bluff above the Mississippi River on the north end of the city, offering panoramic views up and down the river. Amid this river city's 100-year-old sanctuary of forestland, memorial rose gardens, and paved hiking and biking paths are ancient and carefully preserved conical burial mounds in classic placement on a terrace above the river.

James Weed Park

Colorado Street and Park Drive at Highway 22

Muscatine, IA 52761

Directions: From Highway 22 south or north, watch for park signs at the north end of city.

Hours: Open daily.

Helpful Contacts

Muscatine Convention and Visitors Bureau

319 East Second Street, Suite 102

Muscatine, IA 52761

563-263-8895 or 800-257-3275

www.meetmuscatine.com

(37) ALBANY MOUNDS STATE HISTORIC SITE
Albany, IL

The Albany Mounds are sited on a high ridge just north of the confluence of Wapsipinicon River where it flows into the Mississippi. They make up the largest grouping of burial mounds in the state of Illinois. The mounds, over two thousand years old, were built in the Middle Woodland period by the Hopewell people who moved through the Iowa–Illinois region for trade and farming. There were once over eighty mounds; some fifty now remain. The mounds were subjected to extensive archaeological research in the past century but today are held as a national cultural treasure.

The 205 acres sheltering the mounds are matched by another 15-acre site across Meredosia Road, an ancient village site that is, like the mounds, overseen by the Illinois Historic Preservation Agency. The Friends of Albany Indian Mounds Foundation works to foster appreciation and raise funds to maintain the ancient mounds.

Interpretive signage can be found along the mowed paths throughout the parkland. Deer are frequently seen in the park, and eagles are seen in the treetops near the riverbanks. Forestland and prairie can be found around the park district.

There is a parking area at the north end of the park, and picnic facilities are available. The Great River Recreation Trail, very popular with bicyclists, runs just next to the park.

Albany Mounds State Historic Site

Cherry Street at 12th Avenue South

Albany, IL 52142

309-887-4335

Directions: *From the Quad Cities:* Go north out of Moline on Highway 84 about 50 miles up the river to Albany. *From Clinton, IA:* Cross east over the Mississippi River on U.S. 30 into Illinois and turn south on Highway 84 (River Road) for 5 miles into Albany; in Albany, turn left on Park Avenue around the city park, take 5th Avenue up the hill, and turn right at the water tower onto Cherry Street to the park entrance.

Hours: Open daily from sunrise to sunset.

Helpful Contacts

Clinton Area Convention and Visitors Bureau

P.O. Box 1024

Clinton, IA 52732-1024

319-242-5702 or 800-828-5702

www.clinton.net/Clinton

West of Chicago

West of *Chicago?* Indeed! Long before Chicago became an established city, ancient peoples of the Upper Midwest traveled, traded, and settled along the many rivers that flow to the Mississippi or into Lake Michigan. The Illinois, the Rock, the Fox, and the Des Plaines Rivers were major migration routes through present-day Illinois, and these peoples left their mark for our eyes to see today in the form of village sites and effigy and burial mounds in their traditional sitings on the terraces and ridges above the flowing water.

(38) BRISCOE MOUNDS
Near Channahon, IL

The Briscoe Mounds, found on a prominent rise above the Des Plaines River at its confluence with the Kankakee River in the community of Channahon, are the largest burial mounds in northern Illinois and stand in a district well researched for early habitation. Significant village sites are known in the Channahon area that had once in-cluded large plazas, many earth lodges, and perhaps a dozen mounds. Dating on the Briscoe Mounds shows construction between 100 and 1200 c.e. in the Mississippian period.

The mounds site is owned by the Illinois State Museum. Plans are in place for a museum and interpretive center that would highlight the prehistoric times of the district as well as the importance of the Illinois and Michigan Canal just to the south of Channahon.

Briscoe Mounds

Front Street

Channahon, IL 60410

Directions: *From Chicago:* Take I-80 west to I-55 south, take the next exit at Bluff Road, turn right and head west to Eames Street (U.S. 6), pass through the village, go six blocks to Canal Street (the last street before crossing the river), turn left and go all the way to the river, and turn left onto Front Street to the riverbank.

Hours: Open daily.

Helpful Contacts

Village of Channahon

24441 West Eames Street

Channahon, IL 60410

815-467-6644

info@channahon.org

www.channahon.org

(39) OAKWOOD CEMETERY

Joliet, IL

Oakwood Cemetery shelters a low, broad burial mound related in time to the Briscoe Mounds of one thousand years ago. This sole mound, found in the center rear of the cemetery, on a rise above a small creek tributary of the nearby Des Plaines River, was excavated in 1928 by archaeologists of the University of Chicago, who removed over one hundred of the three hundred skeletons inside. These ancient remains have been returned to tribal communities under the Native American Graves Protection and Repatriation Act. The prehistoric earthwork in Higginbotham Woods Forest Preserve is just nearby.

Oakwood Cemetery
East Cass Street
Joliet, IL 60432
Directions: *From Chicago:* Take I-80 west to Joliet, exit at U.S. 30 (Cass Street) and turn left to head west into Joliet, crossing North Briggs Street; the entrance to the cemetery is seven blocks ahead at Walnut Street.

(40) HIGGINBOTHAM WOODS FOREST PRESERVE
Joliet, IL

The Higginbotham Woods Forest Preserve shelters a large irregularly shaped earthwork, possibly the last of its kind that once stood along the high banks of the Illinois and Des Plaines Rivers. Though the embankment has not been dated, it is understood to be of the same Hopewell period as many of the other mounds and village sites in this riverine district (the Oakwood Cemetery mound just nearby is of the same era).

The preserve itself is part of the Joliet Park District and is adjacent to Pilcher Park, a sizable acreage of city recreation land with a nature center and hiking trails. With Will County's recent purchase of the 114-acre Potawatomi Woods as a buffer to Higginbotham Woods Forest Preserve, the region will retain an authentic remnant of wetlands and floodplain in central Joliet, with its archaeological evidence of prehistoric settlement and burial sites.

Higginbotham Woods Forest Preserve

Gougar Road at West Francis Road
Joliet, IL 60432
815-741-7275 (Joliet Park District)
Directions: *From Chicago:* Take I-80 west to Joliet, exit at U.S. 30 (Cass Street) and turn left to head west into Joliet, take the next right turn on Gougar Road, and drive north to the park entrance at West Francis Road.
Hours: Open daily.

Helpful Contacts

Heritage Corridor Convention and Visitor Bureau
81 North Chicago Street
Joliet, IL 60432
(800) 926-CANAL
www.heritagecorridorcvb.com/joliet/jhistory-landmarks.htm

(41) WINFIELD MOUNDS FOREST PRESERVE

Winfield, IL

The Winfield Mounds Forest Preserve shelters three low, circular mounds set in a triangular pattern on a high bank of the West Branch of the DuPage River. The ancient mounds, some one thousand years old, are surrounded by the evidence of a rich village life on the river: archaeologists have found the remains of small crops, wooden fishing weirs, bone fishhooks, berries, nuts, and maple sugaring.

The DuPage County Forest Preserve District made the first land acquisition in 1970 and has since built the preserve to a 360-acre tract. Considerable investigation into the mounds took place in the last century, and there has since been some reconstruction of the mounds. Construction of a footpath trail from the Geneva Spur of the Illinois Prairie Path and the clearing of the area around the mounds for easier observation are being undertaken. Guided tours are available at certain times of the year; call the Forest Preserve District office for information.

Winfield Mounds Forest Preserve
Winfield Road
Winfield, IL 60190
630-933-7200 (DuPage County Forest Preserve District)
www.dupageforest.com/preserves/winfieldmounds.html
Directions: *From Chicago:* Take I-355 north or south to Roosevelt Road (Highway 38), go west 10 miles through Glen Ellyn and Wheaton to Winfield Road, turn north, and cross High Lake Road; the entrance to the preserve will be on the left.
Hours: Open daily from sunrise to sunset.

(42) BEATTIE PARK MOUNDS
Rockford, IL

The Beattie Park effigy mounds—a turtle mound, a linear mound, and two small conical mounds—are sheltered in a square city park on the west bank of the Rock River in downtown Rockford. The mounds are accessible to the public and easily approached. The issue of accessibility has been of increasing concern both to the city of Rockford and to the Sauk Nation, which has convened annual "'Honor the Mounds' Days" each August at the park. The Burpee Museum of Natural History sponsors the Native American Awareness Committee, a partnership of twenty-five community and tribal representatives who are working to raise awareness of the sacred nature of the mounds and to develop interpretive and preservation plans.

Beattie Park

North Main Street at Park Avenue

Rockford, IL 61101

Directions: *From Chicago:* Take I-90 west to I-39/20/51 southwest, take the first exit over the Rock River to Highway 2 (Main Street) north, and drive into Rockford; Main Street comes to a T intersection at Beattie Park.

Hours: Open daily.

Helpful Contacts

Burpee Museum of Natural History

737 North Main Street

Rockford, IL 61103-6971

815-965-3433

www.burpee.org/info.htm

Rockford Area Convention and Visitors Center

211 North Main Street

Rockford, IL 61101

815-963-8111 or 800-521-0849

info@gorockford.com

www.gorockford.com

Milwaukee and the
Lower Rock River

The southeastern district of Wisconsin is dominated by three elements: Lake Michigan, the lower Rock River drainage, and the south unit of the Kettle Moraine State Forest, 21,000 acres of woodland and lakes spanning three counties in southeastern Wisconsin. The Kettle Moraine is a 100-mile band of forested hills, ridges, and depressions in eastern Wisconsin formed along the intersection of two glaciers during the last Ice Age, 10,000 to 25,000 years ago. The district is named for the "kettles," where blocks of melted ice once buried under sand and gravel left deep impressions in the topography, and for the moraines—ridges of mounded sand that formed along the glacier edges.

The state of Wisconsin recognized the unique nature of the district and named it a state forest in 1937. Today the state forest, divided into north and south units, holds 51 miles of bridle trails, more than 20 miles of mountain bike trails, 30 miles of cross-country ski trails, and 46 miles of snowmobile trails. Along with four other marked trails, hikers will find a 32-mile stretch of the Ice Age Hiking Trail. A paved trail is popular with mobility-impaired visitors.

On either side of this vast prehistoric geological formation is water—an inland sea in the form of Lake Michigan and a massive drainage system of creeks and streams flowing out of Wisconsin's Lake Winnebago in the north of the state all the way to the Mississippi River in a delta below Rock Island, Illinois. The entire district was once filled with countless mounds—conical burial and, most especially, effigy—but most are gone now, lost to the last century's rush to development and an undervaluation of the priceless cultural heritage at hand. It is estimated that some twenty thousand mounds once existed, of which perhaps three thousand remain. A considerable number of the mounds once stood within the precincts of present-day Milwaukee, which surprises many visitors; today, the priceless survey maps left by Increase Lapham and Jacob Brower give testimony to the inheritance now lost. There are still many existing examples of these beautiful sites throughout the state, and we will visit some very good ones in southeastern Wisconsin.

Helpful Contacts

Ice Age National Scenic Trail

www.nps.gov/iatr/expanded/history.htm
Kettle Moraine State Forest—Southern Unit
S91 W 39091 Highway 59
Eagle, WI 53119
262-594-6200
www.dnearstate.wi.us/org/land/Forestry/StateForests/meet.htm
#KettleMoraine

(43) BELOIT COLLEGE MOUNDS

Beloit, WI

A wonderfully preserved group of effigy mounds can be found at the south end of the Beloit College campus grounds, which is sited on a rise above the Rock River just by Turtle Creek. The low mounds have long been cherished by Wisconsin's oldest liberal arts college (est. 1846), which has worked to foster a strong stewardship sensibility about the cultural heritage of the district. This has been intentionally underscored with a strong partnership with the Ho-Chunk Nation and with the establishment of a first-class museum of anthropology with a faculty specialization on Upper Midwest peoples and culture.

Twenty-three effigy animal, conical, and linear mounds dated between 700 and 1200 C.E. can be found within the boundaries of the 40-acre campus in the center of the city. One effigy mound is in the shape of a turtle, which has been adopted as a mascot symbol for the college. Visitors can obtain brochures for a self-guided walking tour of the campus from the Administration Office or by contacting the Beloit Visitors Bureau.

Beloit College Mounds

700 College Street

Beloit, WI 53511

608-363-2000

www.beloit.edu

Directions: *From Chicago:* Take I-90 to the South Beloit exit, continue west to Park Avenue, turn right and continue up the hill, and turn left on Chapin Street to College Street. *From Milwaukee:* Take I-43 into Beloit where it becomes Milwaukee Road.

Continue into Beloit and bear left after the railroad tracks to remain on Milwaukee Road. Continue to Chapin Street and turn right toward the campus six blocks ahead.

Hours: Open daily.

Helpful Contacts

Logan Museum of Anthropology
Beloit College
608-363-2677
www.beloit.edu/~museum/logan

Beloit Convention and Visitors Bureau
608-365-4838 or 800-423-5648
www.visitbeloit.com/visitorinfo.htm

(44) MOUND CEMETERY
Racine, WI

It was common in the Upper Midwest to establish pioneer cemeteries around ancient burial mounds, and Racine's Mound Cemetery is an excellent example of that event. There are fourteen large conical burial mounds within this 42-acre city-owned cemetery, placed in classic siting on high ground above the Root River, close to its confluence with Lake Michigan, and dated to the Woodland period of over one thousand years ago. The cemetery administrators have taken thoughtful care of these prehistoric monuments, hedging many of them in with low plantings to protect them. A commemorative stone shaft was raised close to the largest mound in 1908.

Mound Cemetery

1147 West Boulevard

Racine, WI 53403

262-636-9188

sbedard@cityofracine.org

www.cityofracine.org/cemeteries/cemetery.shtml

Directions: *From Chicago or Milwaukee:* Exit I-90 at County Road
11 (Durand Avenue) and head east into the city, bear a wide
left at Taylor Avenue, turn left at the T intersection with Washington Avenue, and turn right onto West Boulevard; the cemetery gates are on the right.

Hours: Open daily. Tours are available by appointment; contact
the cemetery office on weekday mornings.

Helpful Contacts

Racine County Convention and Visitors Bureau

345 Main Street

Racine, WI 53403-1057

800-C-RACINE

www.racine.org

(45) INDIAN MOUNDS PARK
Whitewater, WI

There is a surprise in this small and very pretty college
town: one of the nation's largest effigy mounds districts,
believed to date from 200 to 1200 c.e. The west side location is something of an anomaly, being near neither a lake
nor a waterway, at least since historic times. The 1.5-acre
park is nicely tended by the city, though the signage is in
some disrepair. As with Sheboygan's effigy mounds park,
the Whitewater park is in the midst of a residential district.

Parking is available across the field along one of the residential streets.

Whitewater is just adjacent to the beautiful Kettle Moraine State Forest and abounds in recreational opportunities. Area tribal communities gather for the Mounds Pow-Wow at the park every September; contact the chamber of commerce for information.

Indian Mounds Park

Indian Mound Parkway at Wildwood Road

Whitewater, WI 53190

Directions: *From Beloit:* Take I-90 north to Janesville, exit on Highway 26 going east just after leaving the city, continue north and take Highway 59 going east just below Milton, take 59 into Whitewater to a T intersection with Main Street (12/89), turn left, and drive west to Indian Mound Parkway. *From Madison or Milwaukee:* Take I-94 to the Highway 26 exit, head south on 26 through Jefferson and Fort Atkinson, take U.S. 12/89 south through Fort Atkinson. The highway becomes Main Street in Whitewater, and Indian Mound Parkway is on the west side of the city. Turn off of Main and drive one block south; watch for small curbside park sign.

Hours: Open daily to sunset.

Helpful Contacts

Whitewater Chamber of Commerce

402 West Main Street

P.O. Box 34

Whitewater, WI 53190-0034

262-473-4005

wacc@idcnet.com

www.whitewaterchamber.com

(46) CARROLL COLLEGE MOUNDS

Waukesha, WI

As with the campus at Beloit, Carroll College in Waukesha shelters a nice grouping of low effigy mounds—birds and turtles, along with conical and linear mounds—on the quad between the historic Administration Building and Main Hall. The campus is on a rise above the Fox River and occupies a long slope that overlooks a valley where the city eventually developed.

Considerable research has been done on the mounds and on this immediate district below the campus, which has been shown to be a district of extensive symmetrical tillage lines for corn, an indication of domestic farming. Inside the city limits there are also at least two known natural springs, which would have been considered sacred sites by ancient peoples. Three large conical burial mounds can be found just nearby at Cutler Park.

Carroll College Mounds

100 North East Avenue

Waukesha, WI 53186

262-547-1211 or 800-CARROLL

www.cc.edu

Directions: *From points east or west:* Take I-94 to the Highway 164 exit, and go south into town. Cross Moreland Boulevard and continue south on North Street (now Highway 18) to Barstow, turn left, and stay on Barstow all the way to College Avenue. Turn left; the Administration Building is on the left at the corner of College and East Avenues.

Hours: Open daily.

Helpful Contacts

Waukesha Area Chamber of Commerce

223 Wisconsin Avenue

Waukesha, WI 53186

262-542-4249

chamber@waukesha.org

www.waukesha.org

(47) CUTLER PARK

Waukesha, WI

Three conical mounds have been preserved in Cutler Park next to the city of Waukesha library. The largest mound is 9 feet high and nearly 65 feet across at the base. Increase Lapham surveyed these mounds in 1840 and conducted excavations that revealed that the central mound had been built atop a rock-lined burial chamber. The city of Waukesha purchased the land in 1902 to protect the mounds.

Cutler Park

Wisconsin Avenue between Maple and Grand Avenues

Waukesha, WI 53186

Directions: *From points east or west:* Take I-94 to the Highway 164 exit, and go south into town. Cross Moreland Boulevard and continue south on North Street (now Highway 18) to Barstow, turn left, and stay on Barstow to Wisconsin Avenue. Turn right; the park is on the left between Grand and Maple.

Hours: Open daily.

Helpful Contacts

Waukesha Public Library
321 Wisconsin Avenue
Waukesha, WI 53186
262-524-3680

(48) JEFFERSON COUNTY INDIAN MOUNDS AND TRAIL PARK, KOSHKONONG MOUNDS COUNTRY CLUB
Near Fort Atkinson, WI

Lake Koshkonong, a widening in the Rock River whose name means "the place where we live," was once a vital fishing and hunting ground for ancient peoples. Numerous paths across the marshes were used to cross to village sites on either bank, and the lake was found to be circled by over five hundred effigy and burial mounds on its extensive shoreline at the time of European exploration.

A small number of the effigy mounds still exist, with most sheltered in deep woodland on private property. There is a delightful exception in the form of a new county park on the east shore of the lake developed in partnership with the Fort Atkinson Historical Society and Jefferson County. The five-acre parcel of land was purchased by a Fort Atkinson private citizen, Hugh Highsmith, who has written extensively on the effigy mound culture of the Lake Koshkonong area. Continuous consultation with the Wisconsin state archaeologist and the Ho-Chunk Nation ensured that the new park was sensitively developed.

The result can be seen at the Jefferson County Indian Mounds and Trail Park, which holds within its boundary part of the group of 1,000-year-old mounds known to researchers as the General Atkinson Mound Group, as well as an Indian trail that was documented by a land surveyor in 1835. Here are eleven linear, conical, bird, and turtle effigy mounds, including one turtle mound that measures 222 feet in length.

Excellent interpretive signage is found at the entrance by the small parking lot. There is a brochure kiosk, but the park is popular—if the box is empty (a sure sign of success), the Fort Atkinson Chamber of Commerce can also provide brochures for the park. The Fort Atkinson Historical Society, based at the Hoard Museum in town, holds over fifteen thousand prehistoric artifacts found in the county representing Old Copper, Woodland, and Mississippian culture.

Just a short way up the road is the Koshkonong Mounds Country Club, with its unique eighteen-hole golf course built around another eleven effigy mounds. The club does not function as a tourist site, but a courtesy call at the clubhouse will usually net you permission to walk the course or, sometimes, borrow a cart to tour the grass-covered mounds.

Jefferson County Indian Mounds and Trail Park
Koshkonong Mounds Road
Fort Atkinson, WI 53538
920-563-3210 or 888-733-3678 (Fort Atkinson Area Chamber of Commerce)
Directions: *From Beloit:* Take I-90 to the Highway 26 exit east of Janesville, continue north on 26 through Milton, watch for a left-side split-off of Old Highway 26 shortly after crossing County Road N, take Old Highway 26 north to Koshkonong Mounds Road, turn left, and drive to the lake and park. *From*

Milwaukee: Take I-94 to the Highway 26 exit, head south on 26 through Jefferson and Fort Atkinson, watch for Old Highway 26 on the right shortly after crossing the Rock River, continue to Koshkonong Mounds Road, turn right, and drive to the lake and park. *From Madison:* Take Highway 12-18 east to Jefferson, take the Highway 26 exit south through Fort Atkinson, watch for Old Highway 26 on the right shortly after crossing the Rock River, continue to Koshkonong Mounds Road, turn right, and drive to the lake and park.

Hours: Open daily from May through October.

Helpful Contacts

Fort Atkinson Historical Society
Hoard Historical Museum
407 Merchants Avenue
Fort Atkinson, WI 53538
920-563-7769
info@hoardmuseum.org
www.hoardmuseum.org

Fort Atkinson Area Chamber of Commerce
244 North Main Street
Fort Atkinson, WI 53538
920-563-3210 or 888-733-3678
fortcham@idcnet.com
www.fortchamber.com/index.htm

Koshkonong Mounds Country Club
W7670 Koshkonong Mounds Road
Fort Atkinson, WI 53538-9508
920-563-2823

(49) PANTHER INTAGLIO
Fort Atkinson, WI

The Panther Intaglio, found along the north bank of the Rock River in Fort Atkinson, is the only "negative" mound known to be in existence from the some dozen that once existed in the Upper Midwest. The word *intaglio* comes from the Italian word for a way of making prints by creating a shallow groove in the printer's plate to hold ink. The 125-foot-long Panther Intaglio was formed by scooping out about a foot of earth to leave a sunken impression of an animal, in this case a panther, or water spirit.

Lapham first noted it in 1850 as one of a group of 1,000-year-old effigy mounds that were later destroyed as the city was built out. In 1919 the Daughters of the American Revolution purchased a lease on the remaining land that holds the intaglio to preserve it.

Panther Intaglio
Highway 106 (Riverside Drive)

Fort Atkinson, WI 53538

Directions: *From Beloit:* Take I-90 to the Highway 26 exit east of Janesville, continue north on 26 through Milton, and cross the Rock River. *From Milwaukee:* Take I-94 to the Highway 26 exit, head south on 26 through Jefferson to Fort Atkinson and the Rock River. *From Madison:* Take Highway 12-18 east to Jefferson, take the Highway 26 exit south to Fort Atkinson and the Rock River. From downtown Fort Atkinson look for Riverside Drive three blocks west of Main Street; turn off of Sherman going southwest. Watch for a historical marker on the right.

Hours: Open daily.

(50) AZTALAN STATE PARK
Near Lake Mills, WI

Unchallengeably one of the most important archaeological sites in the Upper Midwest, Aztalan is vast both in scale and in comprehension. The park shelters a Middle Mississippian village and cultural complex dated between 1000 and 1300 C.E. that was a critical trading division point between ancient peoples passing north or south from the Gulf to the Great Lakes. Built on the west bank of the Crawfish River just north of its confluence with the Rock River, the Aztalan complex was a complete city, an offshoot of the great community at Cahokia down the Mississippi River in present-day Illinois. The compound was surrounded by high wooden palisades with watchtowers, enclosing houses, ceremonial platform mounds, and burial sites.

The new settlers at Aztalan would have found themselves surrounded by the more modest culture of the Woodland people, and relations may not have been comfortable—hence the palisade and the watchtowers. At no time did the Aztalan settlement number more than five hundred people over the two hundred years that the community endured. The end of Aztalan came in fire, with the entirety of the settlement appearing to have been burned to the ground.

Aztalan was first recorded in 1835 by European surveyors who excitedly thought the complex was related to the Aztecs and forever gave a name to the site that is wildly improbable. Lapham mapped the compound in 1850 at a time when the entire complex had not been touched by the plow, but the site waited until 1948 to become a state park.

The park is large, approximately 172 acres in all, of which about 25 percent is woodland. There are good interpretive signs for visitors, hiking trails, and picnic facilities near the parking lot. A brochure for self-guided walking tours is available at the Lake Mills Department of Natural Resources offices. Also, the Lake Mills–Aztalan Historical Society operates the small Aztalan Museum just adjacent to the park, where visitors can see a small collection of Mississippian and Woodland artifacts from the district.

Aztalan State Park

Highway Q

Lake Mills, WI 53549

www.dnr.state.wi.us/org/land/parks/specific/aztalan/index.html

Contact: Wisconsin Department of Natural Resources

Glacial Drumlin State Trail

1213 South Main Street

Lake Mills, WI 53551

920-648-8774

Directions: *From Madison or Milwaukee:* Take I-94 to the Lake Mills exit at Highway 89, go south into Lake Mills, turn east on Lake Street (Highway B), drive about 3 miles, and watch for signs to park.

Hours: Open daily from April through October.

Admission: Free.

Helpful Contacts

Lake Mills–Aztalan Historical Society

Aztalan Museum

N6264 Highway Q

Lake Mills, WI 53549

920-648-4632

Hours: Open on afternoons on Thursdays through Sundays, from May to September.

Admission: Small admission fee.

(51) LAKE KEGONSA STATE PARK

Near Stoughton, WI

Lake Kegonsa, which means "lake of many fishes" in the Ho-Chunk (Winnebago) language, was long an important fishing source for ancient peoples. The state park formed around 342 acres along the lakeshore shelters effigy mounds found in the classic siting on a high ridge above the lake along the park's White Oak Nature Trail. Full recreational facilities and camping are available at the park.

Lake Kegonsa State Park

2405 Door Creek Road

Stoughton, WI 53589

608-873-9695

Directions: *From Madison or Milwaukee:* Take I-90 to the Highway "N" exit (#147) southwest of Madison, head south on "N" a few miles, turn right (west) on Koshkonong Road, and then go south on Door Creek Road to the park entrance.

Helpful Contacts

Greater Madison (Dane County) Convention and
    Visitors Bureau

615 East Washington Avenue

Madison, WI 53703

608-255-2537 or 800-373-6376

gmcvb@visitmadison.com

www.visitmadison.com

The Madison Mounds District

CHAPTER 11

(52) THE MADISON MOUNDS DISTRICT

Any community in the Upper Midwest that can claim at least one remaining prehistoric mounds site should feel good that time and circumstance spared that ancient burial from the ravages of time and human interference. That one community in the Upper Midwest can still shelter twenty (twenty!) distinct and separate effigy mound sites within its municipal borders is spectacular.

The people of Madison, Wisconsin, can make that claim and will tell you that these Middle and Late Woodland mound sites are beloved and cared for, wanted and welcomed, helped and hedged in with every possible legal, academic, and honorary accord that the law and human respect can muster. It is understood that the Madison district, ancient home of the ancestors of the Ho-Chunk (Winnebago), contains the finest and largest effigy mounds anywhere in the world.

In 1996, as a gift to the community, the city of Madison and the State Historical Society of Madison commissioned a Madison Heritage Publication titled "Native American Mounds in Madison and Dane County." Free to the public, the booklet is an elegant piece, twenty pages front to back, graced with fine line drawings and a first-rate foldout map. In the years since publication, countless copies have been distributed by the Madison Historic Preservation Landmarks Commission (see "Helpful Contacts" below). Copies can also be found at Madison area libraries and, of course, at the Wisconsin Historical Society in downtown Madison.

Wisconsin's capital city lies at the confluence of Interstates 90 and 94, making travel to Madison easy from Chicago, Milwaukee, or any points north and west in the state. A good city map such as can be purchased from any Madison bookshop or auto service station will give you the layout of this small city beautifully situated on Lakes Mendota and Monona. The street locations of the following recommended effigy mound sites are noted below.

Helpful Contacts

Madison Historic Preservation Landmarks Commission
City of Madison Planning and Development
608-266-6552

Madison Trust for Historic Preservation
P.O. Box 296
Madison, WI 53701-0296
608-256-5941

thetrust@madisontrust.org

www.madisontrust.org/news/dairybarn_central.html

(52-1) BURROWS PARK

A bird effigy mound with a wingspan of 128 feet is on a rise just east of the parking lot on Burrows Road off of Sherman Avenue. A running fox effigy is known to have once existed north of this bird.

(52-2) ELMSIDE PARK

Two effigies thought to be a bear and a lynx can be found on a rise above Lake Monona at the corner of Lakeland and Maple Avenues, all that remains of a much larger group of mounds that once extended down the Yahara River. Harry Whitehorse's sculpture *Let the Great Spirits Soar* honors his Ho-Chunk (Winnebago) ancestors who lived in the district for hundreds of years.

(52-3) HUDSON PARK

This water spirit mound—perhaps a turtle, lizard, or panther—found at the intersection of Lakeland and Hudson Avenues suffered damage to its tail when Lakeland Avenue was built through the area. It was likely once part of the nearby Elmside mounds group.

(52-4) EDNA TAYLOR CONSERVANCY

These six long, linear mounds and a panther effigy are located on a rise off a pathway in a marsh preserve off of Femrite Drive just east of Monona Drive. Start at the trailhead by the parking lot and walk in along the main path; the linears will extend alongside the path, and the panther effigy will be seen on the right just beyond.

(52-5) MENDOTA STATE HOSPITAL GROUNDS

There are two mound groups here, both on the hospital grounds at the intersection of Troy Drive and Green Avenue on the north shore of Lake Mendota. The Mendota State Hospital Group is thought to contain the finest and largest effigy mounds known, including three massive birds, one of which has a wingspan of over 624 feet. Two panther or turtle mounds and one deer effigy are here, as well as two bears, several conicals, and one additional undetermined shape that would appear to have been part of a larger group. The hospital's logo uses the bird effigy imagery.

The Farwell's Point Group is west of the first group, out on a point of land above the lake with a panoramic view of the lake. Here are large and small conicals, the remains of a few linears and panthers, and a bird: the rest of the mounds that were once here were destroyed when the hospital buildings and drives were put in. Research has found numerous village sites and the remains of ancient corn rows here. A recent aerial photo survey points to the probability that the turtle, deer, and bird are aligned to correspond to the moon, the sun, and the North Star.

Check in at the desk at the Administration Building off of Troy Drive, the first building on the right. The hospital will provide you with a map of the grounds.

(52-6) CHEROKEE PARK

This park shelters two large conical mounds a bit off the main paths. To reach the first mound, starting at the parking lot near the north end of Sherman Avenue, walk in on the service drive and take the third right turn onto the gravel trail just before the "Service Drive" sign. To reach the second mound, start out the same way but take the second right turn, the next left, the next right and then walk up to the mound near the top of the hill (the woods will be on the left).

(52-7) VILAS CIRCLE PARK

This small oval park in the middle of Vilas Avenue preserves a large bear effigy, once part of a larger group of a second bear, a conical, and seven linear mounds. The park is on a curve of Vilas at the bottom of Randall Avenue.

(52-8) VILAS PARK

You can find a bird effigy and a linear and conical mound each on the corner of Erin and Wingra Streets overlooking the city zoo. Of note is a commemorative plaque placed in 1915 in a ceremony attended by twelve tribal community representatives. As you gaze out over the zoo remember that much of the district below was originally marshland and rich hunting and ricing grounds.

(52-9) FOREST HILL CEMETERY

As we have learned, it happened often that the pioneer cemeteries of the last centuries were formed around the many ancient burial monuments that were already here at the time of European settlement. In the lovely Forest Hill Cemetery at the intersection of Regent Street, Highland Avenue and Speedway Road are two panther effigies and a linear and—unusual—goose effigy each (unfortunately the head of the goose was lopped off when the Illinois Central came through in the 1880s). To reach the mounds from the main entrance, follow the left-most forks in the road until you have reached the back of the cemetery near the railroad tracks. You can pick up a map of the grounds as a guide from the cemetery office during weekday hours.

(52-10) EDGEWOOD COLLEGE CAMPUS

Twelve mounds can be found on the campus overlooking Lake Wingra, once a large ricing marsh. Take Edgewood Drive along the lakeshore to see seven conicals and the end of a linear. There are two partial linear mounds between Edgewood Drive and the college library, and on the other side of the library is a large bird effigy. Two more conicals can be found alongside a path to the north of the grade-school playground. A final mound, a remnant of one of two bear effigies that were known to be here, can be seen by the northeast wall of the Student Services Building.

(52-11) OBSERVATORY HILL

On Observatory Drive, near the crest of Observatory Hill and to the west of the observatory building, are a bird and a turtle effigy each. The bird's wings have lost some length, and the turtle is known to have had a rare forked tail, but they are all but gone now. The nearby plaque has an error in the dating: We now know that the mounds are significantly older than was once thought.

(52-12) WILLOW DRIVE

On the north side of the natatorium is a group of effigies; one is known to be a goose, but the other two beyond the goose remain undefined. The wings of the goose were once bent, but the early construction of Willow Drive destroyed part of the effigy. Reach Willow Drive from Observatory Drive.

(52-13) PICNIC POINT

Two linear and three conical mounds can be found halfway down the pedestrian path that leads to the tip of Picnic Point from Willow Drive on Lake Mendota's southern shore. Another group of effigies was destroyed by plowing when this area was farmland.

(52-14) THE UNIVERSITY OF WISCONSIN ARBORETUM

There are two effigy mound groups on both sides of the main drive into the Arboretum. From Seminole Highway, take McCaffrey Drive to the parking lot on the right. The first mound group is reached on the pedestrian path by the sign at the northeast corner of the lot: on either side of the main path, just beyond the first right-hand path, are conicals and linears. Back up to the first right-hand path and walk on to see a panther effigy and linear on the left of the path and a conical and a bird mound on the right. There are two more linears beyond the next intersection. The Arboretum, 1,260 acres bordering the southern half of Lake Wingra, is open daily.

(52-15) SPRING HARBOR SCHOOL GROUNDS

One bear mound can be found on the Spring Harbor School campus north of the school building on Lake Mendota Drive, one of the last of an immense group of mounds that existed on this part of the Lake Mendota shoreline.

(52-16) GOVERNOR NELSON STATE PARK

This group overlooking the north shore of Lake Mendota consists of five conical mounds and a panther effigy. The group once included several more panthers and a bird effigy. A self-guided tour brochure can be picked up at the park office off of County Trunk Highway M. Take Indianola Trail from the main park entrance, bear south, and follow the Indianola–Wakanda Trail loop. The mounds can be found on the eastern end of the loop near the southern end of the trail. There is a day fee that can be paid at the park office; visitors intending to stay only a short time can get passes for an hour.

(52-17) YAHARA HEIGHTS COUNTY PARK

These effigies, a bear and panther and a conical, are on a rise above the Yahara River and surrounding marshland. The panther is quite large, measuring 228 feet. From the park gates at the corner of Riverview Drive and Caton Lane, take the main trail and watch for the panther; the bear is several hundred feet beyond to the north.

(52-18) INDIAN MOUND PARK

This park sits on a ridge overlooking Lake Waubesa and Mud Lake. From the park entrance on Burma Road follow the walking trail southward. This will take you past the remnant of a linear mound, then a conical and an elliptical, a bear effigy, another linear, and an uncommonly shaped hook mound that is thought to have possibly been the curved tail of a panther or water spirit effigy. Though the mounds have never been harmed by plow or backhoe, considerable visitation created wear on the mounds, and the community of McFarland has assumed stewardship of them, working to restore the original condition of the effigies and reroute the walking paths.

(52-19) GOODLAND COUNTY PARK

A group of three linear mounds and a conical mound can be found on both sides of the main road toward the west shore of Lake Waubesa. Reach the park from Waubesa Avenue

(52-20) SIGGELKOW PARK

This park off of U.S. 51 shelters a long linear mound about 225 feet long on the top of a hill overlooking Lake Waubesa and Mud Lake. Park on Rustic Way just south of Sigglekow Road and hike to the top of the hill. There are known to be remnants of other linear mounds nearby.

CHAPTER 12

The Wisconsin River Valley

Running straight down the center of the state, the great Wisconsin River carries a majestic geologic and cultural history on its 500-mile journey from the Michigan border to the Mississippi River at Prairie du Chien, dropping 1,000 feet through the river gorges it carved during the Ice Age. The state took its name from the Ojibwe word for the river, Wees-kon-san, "the gathering of the waters."

The passage of the river from the Wisconsin Rapids to the Wisconsin Dells has a special aspect: the tangible reminder of an ancient people in the symbols they left us in their burial and effigy mounds and in their rock art—carvings and paintings on stone—in the massive bluffs that characterize the middle reaches of this river. In this district the traveler will find great water spirit effigies and high conicals overlooking quiet backwater meadows of the great river, as well as the only rock art site open to the public in the state of Wisconsin.

(53) LAKESIDE PARK AND THE GOTTSCHALL CAVE
Avoca, WI

A group of ten Late Woodland mounds—six linear and four conical—is found in Lakeside Park and campground above the shore of Avoca Lake, a long slender backwater slough formed by a tributary stream to the south bank of the Wisconsin River.

Also in the Avoca area is one of Wisconsin's great archaeological treasures, the Gottschall Rockshelter. This remarkable site holds magnificent pictographs reflecting the Ho-Chunk Red Horn legend and has been the subject of study by Dr. Robert Salzer for more than a decade. Visitors to Gottschall come from all over the world to see this remarkable site. Tours are available by arrangement.

Dr. Salzer has also spearheaded the formation of a new nonprofit educational foundation, Cultural Landscapes Legacies, Inc. (CLL), in partnership with the Lower Wisconsin State Riverway Board and many other tribal and community leaders on the Wisconsin River. CCL is designed as a land trust dedicated to provide for education, preservation, and protection of the cultural landscapes of the indigenous peoples of the Upper Midwest. A self-guided "Effigy Mound Grand Tour" brochure is available by contacting Dr. Salzer.

Lakeside Park

East Lake Shore Drive

Avoca, WI 53506

Directions: State Highway 133 becomes Main Street in Avoca, turn north onto 1st Street to Lakeshore Drive, turn right, and drive east to the park.

The Gottschall Rockshelter
Cultural Landscapes Legacies, Inc.
Dr. Robert Salzer
2943 South Nye School Road
Beloit, WI 53511-8649
Beloit: 608-362-8812
Avoca: 608-532-6385

(54) WISCONSIN HEIGHTS BATTLE SITE
Near Sauk City, WI

The Wisconsin Department of Natural Resources (DNR) has developed an interpretive trail commemorating the Battle of Wisconsin Heights, a terrible conflict between territorial militia and the fleeing Sac and Fox Nation led by Black Hawk in summer 1832. Wisconsin Heights is the name given to a bluff on the Wisconsin River a few miles below Sauk City. The land comprising what has been familiarly called the Black Hawk Prairie at Wisconsin Heights for many years was purchased by the DNR in 1990 and—through a partnership of the DNR and the Sac and Fox Nation now on reservations in Iowa, Kansas, and Oklahoma—has been meticulously restored to its original prairie and oak savannah.

The historic era is represented with marked trails interpreting the event of the battle and noting the many ancient "marker trees" that had been formed and bent in shape as they grew to intentionally point in certain directions. The prehistoric era is also well represented in the form of effigy mounds—a bird, a bear, and two panthers—preserved and studied in partnership with the Ho-Chunk (Winnebago) Nation and found down the river near the Wisconsin Heights battle site.

The entire district is now well along in development for an interpretive park with hiking trails and educational programs. Though there is no local contact or much online information available at this time, interested visitors wanting more news about the Wisconsin Heights Battle Site development plan and history can contact the Wisconsin DNR offices in Madison.

Wisconsin Heights Battlefield Site

County Road Y and Highway 78
Sauk City, WI 53583

Directions: *From Madison:* Take either Highway 12/14 or Highway 19 west to 12/19, continue north to the intersection with Highway 78 just below Sauk Rapids, turn south onto 78, and watch for the park sign 4 miles southeast, near the junction of County Road Y.

Helpful Contacts

Wisconsin Department of Natural Resources
101 South Webster Street
Madison, WI 53703
608-266-2621

Sauk Prairie Area Chamber of Commerce
207 Water Street, Suite D
Sauk City, WI 53583
608-643-4168 or 800-68-EAGLE
www.saukprairie.com

"The Black Hawk War of 1832" (an excellent educational piece)
http://lincoln.lib.niu.edu/blackhawk/page2c.html

(55) DEVIL'S LAKE STATE PARK

Near Baraboo, WI

Devil's Lake State Park is one of Wisconsin's most popular recreation destinations, sited just north of Lake Wisconsin, a broad opening in the Wisconsin River, and up a small tributary creek that once flowed from Devil's Lake and has now been geologically isolated, leaving the lake behind. The lake is spring fed and surrounded by sheer 500-foot cliffs. The area around the lake was visited by ancient peoples for thousands of years. At one time there were hundreds of burial and effigy mounds in the area, but today the remaining nine effigies are inside the park boundaries.

The name "Devil's Lake" is a mistranslation of the Ho-Chunk name Tamahcunchukdah, or Sacred Lake. Ho-Chunk tradition tells us that the great bluffs around the body of water were created during a battle between the Thunderbirds and the Water Spirits. The effigy mounds we can see here are only a fraction of what was once found on these lakeshores (and have been rebuilt somewhat), but they can still show us a part of that story: there is a 150-foot-long fork-tailed bird on the southeastern shore of the lake, and effigies from the opposing "lower world," including a bear and a panther, or water spirit, can be found at the northern end of the lake.

As of the last visit, the park's effigy mounds were unprotected and showed wear from many years of climbing feet. With a renewed investment in the protection of Wisconsin's antiquities, it is likely that a partnership between the state and the many tribal nations that honor these mounds will result in a new plan to more closely shelter the mounds from further destruction.

The park has all the expected recreational amenities,

including nearly thirty miles of hiking trails and a nature interpretive trail. The Visitors Center has some interpretive exhibits illustrating the prehistoric aspects of the park.

Devil's Lake State Park

S5975 Park Road

Baraboo, WI 53913-9299

608-356-8301

www.dnearstate.wi.us/org/land/parks/specific/devilslake/
   index.html

Directions: *From Baraboo:* Follow Highway 123 south to the park entrance.

Hours: Open daily.

Admission: There are state parks admission and camping fees.

Helpful Contacts

"Devil's Lake State Park Visitor's Guide: Ancient Earthworks"
www.devilslake.org/mounds.html

Baraboo Area Chamber of Commerce

P.O. Box 442

Baraboo, WI 53913

608-356-8333 or 800-BARABOO

visitus@baraboo.com

www.baraboo.com/chamber

(56) MAN MOUND COUNTY PARK

Near Baraboo, WI

The Man Mound effigy found just northeast of the city of Baraboo is the only remaining human effigy figure known among Wisconsin's many effigy mounds. It is not uncommon to find human figures, or hands, carved or painted on rock in this district, but no other human-form earthwork remains.

Increase Lapham and William Canfield found the effigy virtually intact at 214 feet at the foot of a high ridge when they surveyed it in 1859. Today it is preserved on a modest acreage of land in Sauk County, having lost the feet and the lower legs from road construction in 1905.

The mound, dated to about one thousand years ago, is built to show a striding figure wearing a horned headpiece as would be traditional of Native American shamans. It can be viewed from an elevated platform built adjacent to the mound.

Man Mound County Park
Man Mound Road
Baraboo, WI 53913
608-546-5011
Directions: *From Baraboo:* Drive east on Highway 33, turn left on County Road T, and then turn right on Man Mound Road.
Hours: Open daily.

(57) KINGSLEY BEND MOUNDS
Near Wisconsin Dells, WI

The Kingsley Bend mound group, now sheltered in an attractive state highway roadside rest stop, is found along an ancient run of the Wisconsin River, filled with horseshoe bends and small islands below the famous rock formations and canyons of the Wisconsin Dells. This is, in the minds of many, one of the most exceptional geological districts in the state of Wisconsin.

The Kingsley Bend mounds include a massive panther or water spirit effigy of extraordinary length, a bird with a

200-foot wingspan, two 100-foot-long bears, and several high conicals and long linears, all built between 700 and 1000 c.e. and found on a high shelf overlooking the slow-moving water meadows of the river. There are many other effigy mounds known in the immediate district, but they are protected on private land. Though the mounds are unfenced, the Kingsley Bend effigies show remarkably little wear from foot traffic.

The rest area has plenty of room for parking, and there are pleasant picnic facilities on the lawns. The district around the park has many other historic and prehistoric sites to visit, including the Wauona Trail, the portage route between the Fox and Wisconsin Rivers, now a National Historic Landmark. The fabulously popular Wisconsin Dells recreational district is just up the road.

Kingsley Bend Mounds

State Highway 16

Wisconsin Dells, WI 53965

www.co.columbia.wi.us/history/mounds.asp

Directions: *From Wisconsin Dells or Portage:* Take Highway 16 to the Kingsley Bend Wayside about 4 miles below Wisconsin Dells.

Hours: Open daily.

Helpful Contacts

Columbia County Visitors Bureau

311 East Wisconsin Street, Suite 108

Portage, WI 53901

800-842-2524

http://fun.co.columbia.wi.us/fun/history/default.asp

Wisconsin Dells Visitor and Convention Bureau
701 Superior Street
Wisconsin Dells, WI 53965
800-223-3557
www.wisdells.com

(58) GEE'S SLOUGH (NEW LISBON) MOUNDS
Near New Lisbon, WI

The effigy mounds south of the present-day community of New Lisbon are found on a bank above a small backwater of the Lemonweir River, a large tributary of the Wisconsin River. The New Lisbon area was a gathering place for the earlier Woodland peoples and remained so for the historic Ho-Chunk Nation after European settlement.

The Gee's Slough mound group holds several conical and linear mounds as well as a long-tailed running panther (water spirit), unusual for its flexed legs. These effigy mounds, set out in a small park setting, have been under the protection of the community for a long time, originally having been on the private property of the Bailey family and then having been given over to the stewardship of the New Lisbon Lion's Club, which undertook the restoration and continuing care of the site and placed a historical marker just off the roadside with information about the mounds.

While there are numerous petroglyphs throughout the Lemonweir River district, these images are on private property and are under the care of the State Historical Society of Wisconsin and the Ho-Chunk Nation. However, you can see castings of these rock art images and many local Woodland artifacts at the public library in town.

Gee's Slough (New Lisbon) Mounds

Indian Mound Road

New Lisbon, WI 53950

Directions: *East from Tomah or west from Wisconsin Dells:* Take I-90/94 to the New Lisbon exit (Highway 80), take 80 south through town to connect with Highway 12/16, and turn left on Indian Mound Road just after the railroad tracks.

Hours: Open daily from April through October.

Helpful Contacts

New Lisbon Chamber of Commerce

800 German Town Road, P.O. Box 79

New Lisbon, WI 53950

608-562-3555

nlchambr@mwt.net

www.homestead.com/newlisbonchamber

Hours: Open on weekday mornings.

New Lisbon Memorial Library

115 West Park Street

New Lisbon, WI 53950

608-562-3213

Hours: Open on Monday through Saturday; call for hours.

(59) CRANBERRY CREEK MOUND GROUP

Near Necedah, WI

The Cranberry Creek mounds are in a Wisconsin Department of Natural Resources State Natural Area set-aside of floodplain forest above a channel of Cranberry Creek, a small tributary among hundreds that flows into the Yellow River, which itself then joins the Wisconsin River at Castle

Rock Lake. Surveying and mapping of the area have been ongoing since the early part of the century, but it is only recently that some of the mounds in the preserve have been made available for public observation.

This Woodland mound group, considered one of the largest and best-preserved complexes in the Upper Midwest, holds a great range of the known effigy symbols found in Wisconsin, including conicals, ovals, linears, panther (water spirit) effigies, and a bird effigy with a wingspan of 125 feet. The mounds are not fully cleared, and visitors can see the mounds as they first might have been found by European settlers centuries ago.

The Cranberry Creek preserve is deep in heavily wooded and boggy terrain, down a long dirt road. Passage down this road can be difficult for smaller vehicles or vans with low clearance. There is no parking area; vehicles must be left out on the county road intersection while visitors hike in the half mile. Hiking boots are recommended, as well as bug spray and bottled water for hot summer days. The preserve is very large (458 acres); hikers should stay together.

Cranberry Creek Mound Group, State Natural Area No. 203

7th Street

Necedah, WI 54646

Directions: *From Tomah:* If traveling I-94, leave Tomah at the Highway 21 exit and drive east into Necedah, take County Road G shortly after leaving the town limits, and drive north about 10 miles to the intersection with County Road F and 7th Street. Visitors can park at the roadside along the rail fence or bring their vehicles down the road (not recommended).

Hours: Open daily from late spring through October.

Helpful Contacts

Wisconsin Department of Natural Resources
101 South Webster Street
Madison, WI 53703
608-266-2621

Juneau County Historical Society
P.O. Box 321
Mauston, WI 53948
608-462-5931

(60) ROCHE-A-CRI STATE PARK
Near Friendship, WI

The wonderful name for this small state park comes from the French for "crevice in the rock," and a more appropriate name could not have been found for this wonderland of wind- and glacier-shaped sandstone, a 300-foot-high outcropping that was once an island in the midst of ancient glacial Lake Wisconsin. The outcropping, the very heart of the park, is covered with extraordinary petroglyphs (carvings) and pictographs (paintings) left by the early peoples of Wisconsin over the last thousand years. The petroglyphs came first, sometime around 100 c.e., and the paintings came about five hundred years later.

Roche-A-Cri surely held great ceremonial significance, not just because it was a physically magnificent monument but also because the rock faces of bluffs were thought to be doors to the spirit world. Among the many rock art symbols that can be seen at Roche-A-Cri are moons, starbursts, thunderbird ("turkey") tracks, and a panther, or water spirit. The visitor will see considerable historic carvings and graffiti among the prehistoric symbols.

A 303-step white oak stairway takes visitors past two rest areas on the way up to an observation deck with interpretive signage that permits visitors to view—but not touch!—the many images found on the rock face. Roche-A-Cri, though one of the smaller state parks at 411 acres, offers a full range of recreational opportunities, including miles of hiking trails and wooded campsites.

Roche-A-Cri State Park

1767 Highway 13

Friendship, WI 53934

608-339-6881

www.dnearstate.wi.us/org/land/parks/specific/roche-a-cri/index.htm

Directions: About 22 miles north from the Wisconsin Dells or 25 miles south from Wisconsin Rapids on State Highway 13, the park is just north of the towns of Friendship and Adams. Travelers on I-90/94 should take the Highway 82 exit at Mauston and then go 10 miles east to Highway 13 and north about 12 miles to the park.

Hours: Open daily from May through October.

Admission: There are state park and camping fees.

Helpful Contacts

Adams County Chamber of Commerce

115 South Main Street, P.O. Box 576

Adams, WI 53910

608-339-6997 or 888-339-6997

adamsccc@maqs.net

www.adamscountywi.com/chamber/ancienthistory.htm

(61) WHISTLER INDIAN MOUNDS PARK
Hancock, WI

The Whistler mounds group, a Late Woodland series dating from 500 to 1200 C.E., is located between Pine and Fish Lakes just east of the village of Hancock. These fourteen mounds, once a part of a group of about seventy, include a double-walled oval enclosure as well as two straight lines of low conical mounds. Enclosure mounds are thought to have defined ceremonial sacred spaces. Such enclosure mounds were once found across a broad range of the northeastern United States, but the Whistler enclosure mound is one of the very few to have escaped destruction from plowing or development.

The Village of Hancock is continuing to develop the parkland around the mounds to include careful grooming of the mounds themselves, the development of trails and an interpretive center, and the acquisition of adjacent wetlands for nature trails. This ensures that the Whistler mound group will be the first in Waushara County to be preserved and interpreted for the public. A brochure for a self-guided walking tour is available at the Hancock Public Library.

Whistler Indian Mounds Park
County Road FF
Hancock, WI 54943
715-249-5521 (Town of Hancock)
Directions: Go about 35 miles north from Portage or 28 miles south from Stevens Point on I-39/51 to the village of Hancock, exit at County Road V, drive east, and take County Road FF to park. *From Roche-A-Cri:* Take Highway 13 north to Highway 21, then go west on 21 about 12 miles, turn north on I-39/51 at

Coloma, drive about 6 miles to Hancock, exit at County Road V and drive east, and take County Road FF to park.

Helpful Contacts

Village of Hancock
P.O. Box 154
Hancock, WI 54943
715-249-5521
www.1hancock.com

Hancock Public Library
114 South Main Street, P.O. Box 217
Hancock, WI 54943-0217
715-249-5817

(62) UPPER WHITING PARK
Whiting, WI

The ten ancient burial and effigy mounds on the east bank of the Plover River in the village of Whiting have slept undisturbed for much of the past century since they were first surveyed in the late 1880s. The mounds are in classic placement high on a ridge above the Plover just north of its confluence with the Wisconsin River. Upper Whiting Park is on the Green Circle Trail, the Stevens Point area's 24-mile nature trail of river shores, trees, wild birds, and animals.

The village has recently partnered with the Central Wisconsin Archaeology Center (CWAC) at the University of Wisconsin–Stevens Point to clear and protect the mounds and to provide public interpretation with a recently constructed kiosk describing the cultural and natural history of the area. The archaeologists with the CWAC consider the mounds at Whiting as the most northern extent of the Effigy Mound culture in the state.

Upper Whiting Park

County Road HH (McDill Avenue)

Whiting, WI 54481

Directions: *From Stevens Point:* Take Church or Water Street (Highway 51 Business Route) south across the Plover River and bear left to County Road HH (McDill) to the park.

Hours: Open daily.

Helpful Contacts

Central Wisconsin Archaeology Center

University of Wisconsin–Stevens Point

D314A Science Building

Stevens Point, WI 54481-3897

715-346-4888

cwac@uwsp.edu

www.uwsp.edu/special/cwac

Green Circle Trail

City of Stevens Point

http://stevenspoint.com (click on "A–Z Index of This Site" and on "Green Circle")

(63) LAKE EMILY COUNTY PARK

Amherst Junction, WI

This 143-acre county park west of the village of Amherst Junction occupies the eastern side of Lake Emily and shelters a small collection of effigy mounds. The lake itself is just a short way from the Tomorrow River, which rises in the same wetlands as the Plover River where the Upper Whiting Park mounds can be found.

The mounds were first mentioned in the 1890s when the reports of relic hunters working at the mounds were written up in the *Stevens Point Journal*. Though later reports on the mounds in state archaeological society journals noted the mounds as "an exceptionally fine group" and "worthy of a special effort to preserve them," no special care was taken of the mounds, and some were lost to development. The county park ensures a protected space for the mounds. It has a mile-long nature trail and camping facilities.

Lake Emily County Park
Lake Emily Road
Amherst Junction, WI 54407
715-824-3175 or 715-346-1433 (Portage County Parks)
Directions: *From Stevens Point:* Take U.S. 10 approximately 15 miles west to Amherst Junction, turn left on 2nd Street, and turn left again on Lake Emily Road to park.
Hours: Open daily.

CHAPTER 13

Four Rivers and Points North

Location, location, location! Don't we all love a hilltop and a river view? It has been true for most of human existence. Our last district of archaeology parks makes a visit to some outstanding waterside effigy and burial mound sites, placed just where we would expect to find them: taking in the marvelous view, the fresh air, and the sense of touching the sky from an open and high place above water, close to the stars and the heavens at night.

The Upper Rock, the Fox, the Sheboygan, and the Milwaukee Rivers all have wonderful effigy and burial mound sites, as well as newly discovered petroforms, effigy and celestial shapes outlined with boulders. The last listings in our district take us north, up to the far tip of Door County, and then, finally leaving the Effigy Mound culture, we go around Green Bay and up the shoreline of Lake Michigan, at last ranging up to Michigan's Copper Country to visit two prehistoric Copper culture sites.

(64) LIZARD MOUNDS COUNTY PARK

Near West Bend, WI

Lizard Mounds is one of the best-known archaeology parks in Wisconsin, established in 1950 to preserve a superb grouping of effigy mounds dating from 500 to 1200 C.E. The park takes its name from an enormous effigy that was once called a lizard and is now more familiarly known as a turtle, the ancient symbol of the Earth, which the sacred Turtle carried on his back.

The park contains thirty-one bird, panther (water spirit), turtle, conical, and linear effigies (out of an original grouping of sixty or more) that are threaded by a very well-designed nature trail with interpretive signage. The grounds are beautifully wooded, with oak, maple, beech, and basswood trees.

The park is maintained by Washington County solely for the purpose of preserving the mounds. There is ample parking at the entrance to the park, and picnic and restroom facilities are available.

Lizard Mounds County Park

County Road A

West Bend, WI 53090

262-335-4445 (Washington County Parks)

www.co.washington.wi.us/landuse/Lizard%20Mound.html

Directions: *From West Bend:* Take Highway 144 north 2 miles to County Road A, turn east, and drive one mile to the park entrance at Indian Lore Road. *About 15 miles from Port Washington:* Take Highway 33 west through Newburg to County Road M, drive north to County Road, turn left, and drive to the park entrance at Indian Lore Road.

Hours: Open daily from April through November.

Helpful Contacts

West Bend Area Chamber of Commerce
735 South Main Street, Suite 101
West Bend, WI 53095
262-338-2666 or 888-338-8666
info@wbchamber.org
www.wbchamber.org

(65) HORICON MARSH

Near Mayville, WI

The Horicon Marsh covers over 32,000 acres and is the largest freshwater cattail marsh in the country. It is here that the Rock River rises, gathering waters from tributary streams above the marsh and binding them into a river at the southern confluence.

Long known for its vast migrations of birds and waterfowl, and as a desirable living area in the time of the European pioneers, the marsh has had ancient settlement use and holds many prehistoric secrets in the form of lost village sites and many effigy and burial mound sites long ago recorded and only recently being rediscovered. The Ho-Chunk and Potawatomi have been in this area for many hundreds of years, and it is their ancestors who once lived on the shores of the watery meadow.

Horicon Marsh is flourishing today, but it has passed through some evil chapters, once having been disastrously drained and in grave danger of losing its critical contribution to the health of much of the state's—and the country's—wildlife. Today the marsh is jointly owned by the state of Wisconsin and the Federal Fish and Wildlife Service and is a destination for visitors from around the world who love the great open spaces of the marsh, the rare migrations of bird and butterfly, the long boardwalks, the miles of hiking trails, and the outstanding Visitor Center, with interpretive exhibits on marsh life and history.

The marsh managers, specialists of the Wisconsin Department of Natural Resources (DNR) who are dedicated to the preservation and the fostering of the marsh's many wonders, are carefully overseeing the clearing and protection of a number of effigy mound sites long known to exist on the perimeters of this great water meadow. One effigy mound site is now open to the public along County Road Z, an old Indian trail on a rising bank on the east side of the marsh. Several panther and conical mounds have been cleared and preserved at this wayside stop, and the small park has a lovely serenity with the great marsh just across the road.

If you call ahead you can talk with the refuge's staff naturalist, based at the DNR Service Center on the marsh edge, who is highly knowledgeable about the natural and cultural history of the marsh. There are also excellent maps and interpretive pages on the DNR's Horicon website. Also, a Native American Heritage Weekend is held in late April each year during which visitors can partake of lectures on the marsh's ancient peoples and take guided tours of area archaeological sites.

Horicon Marsh

N7725 Highway 28

Horicon, WI 53032-9782

920-387-7860

volkew@dnearstate.wi.us

www.dnearstate.wi.us/org/land/wildlife/reclands/horicon

Directions: *North from Milwaukee or south from Fond du Lac:* Take U.S. Highway 41 to the exit at Highway 67/County Road H, turn west on H to County Road Z, turn south (left) on Z along the marsh, and watch for the small roadside parking area on the left.

Helpful Contacts

Dodge County Tourism
www.dodgecounty.com/marsh/honk.html
City of Mayville Chamber of Commerce
15 South School Street
Mayville, WI 53050
920-387-7900
www.mayvillecity.com/organizations/chamber.html

City of Horicon Chamber of Commerce
P.O. Box 23
Horicon, WI 53032-0023
920-485-3200
www.horiconchamber.com

(66) INDIAN MOUNDS PARK
Sheboygan, WI

Sheboygan's lovely Indian Mounds Park is sited on a high ridge above a small tributary creek that flows into Lake Michigan south of the city. The site is ideal, being just south of where the Sheboygan River also meets the great inland sea.

The effigies here, known to researchers as the Kletzien Mound Group, are matchlessly cared for by community groups of the city, and great thought has been taken to the development of the interpretation and protection of the eighteen conical, linear, panther, and—very rare—deer effigies in this 15-acre park that lies sheltered in the midst of a quiet residential neighborhood. One of the mounds, excavated earlier in the century, has been encased with Plexiglas to show the burial inside. The mounds have been dated to 500–750 C.E.

A small nature preserve can be found in the glen below, and stairs to the preserve are found at the south end of the park leading down to a boardwalk that wanders through native hardwoods and some rare species of plants. There is ample parking but no picnic facilities here. A guide to the park can be picked up at City Hall.

Indian Mounds Park

9th Street and Panther Avenue
Sheboygan, WI 53081
920-459-3444

Directions: *From I-43 at Sheboygan:* Exit Highway 28 (Washington Avenue) and drive east toward the lake, cross Business Drive and continue another quarter mile, turn right on 12th Street (County Road K), drive two blocks south to Panther Avenue (watch for the park sign on the corner), turn left onto Panther and drive to 9th Street, and turn right into the park entrance.
Hours: Open daily from April through November.

Helpful Contacts

Sheboygan County Convention and Visitors Bureau
712 Riverfront Drive, Suite 101
Sheboygan, WI 53081
800-457-9497 ext. 700

(67) HENSCHEL HOMESTEAD/MUSEUM OF INDIAN HISTORY
Near Elkhart Lake, WI

Elkhart Lake has an ancient history of settlement and ceremony. Early peoples called the lake Ma-Shay-Wa-O-Dey-
Ni-Bas, or "elk heart" for its shape. This 300-acre spring-
fed lake has known the Menomonee, the Sac, the Ojibwe,
and the Potawatomi to have lived near or around it or the
nearby Sheboygan marsh, some well into the time of the
American Civil War.

Many of the village, burial, and ceremonial sites of the
area are well known to the Henschel family, who first
homesteaded here in the mid–nineteenth century, and it is
on their farm that we find a wonderful grouping of effigy
mounds that the Henschel family opens to the public during the summer months. The Henschel family has worked
with state archaeologists to continue to clear and docu-
ment the effigies, and a small museum has been built on
the grounds to provide interpretation and display for many
artifacts found in the district.

Henschel Homestead/Museum of Indian History
N8661 Holstein Road
Elkhart Lake, WI 53020
920-876-3193
Directions: *From Elkhart Lake:* Drive north on Highway 67, turn
left on County Road MM, turn right on County Road J, turn
left on Grogen Road, turn right on Holstein Road, and watch for
the sign.
Hours: Open afternoons on Tuesday through Saturday, from
Memorial Day through Labor Day.
Admission: There is a modest admission fee.

Helpful Contacts

Elkhart Lake Chamber of Commerce
41 East Rhine Street
Elkhart Lake, WI 53020
920-876-2922 or 877-ELKHART
www.elkhartlake.com

(68) CALUMET COUNTY PARK
Near Stockbridge, WI

Lake Winnebago, Wisconsin's largest inland body of water, has always been a nexus for Wisconsin's ancient peoples' travel and trade routes, village sites, and ceremonial and burial sites. This 24-mile-long sheet of water drains two major rivers and countless smaller tributaries and is now home to four major Wisconsin cities. Two large groupings of effigy mounds can be found on the tall cliffs above the lake's eastern shore.

The Calumet County Park shelters six effigies of panthers, or water spirits, in a small county park at the top of the Niagara escarpment overlooking the lake. The 200-acre park offers full recreational and camping opportunities, including extensive hiking trails and a nature center.

Calumet County Park

N6150 County Road EE
Stockbridge, WI 53088
920-439-1008

Directions: *From Appleton and Neenah-Menasha:* Take U.S. 10/114 east to Highway 114 south, turn south on Highway 55 to County Road EE, and drive west to the park entrance.

Helpful Contacts

Calumet County Tourism

P.O. Box 24

Chilton, WI 53014

888-576-9196

www.calumetcountytourism.com

(69) HIGH CLIFF STATE PARK
Near Sherwood, WI

High Cliff, on the northeastern shore of Lake Winnebago, takes its name from the magnificent Niagara escarpment that cuts across this part of the district. The park shelters thirteen large effigy mounds, first surveyed by Increase Lapham in the 1850s, representing birds, buffalo, and panther water spirits, one of which stretches to a length of 285 feet. A half-mile interpretive trail leads up and around the mounds.

High Cliff represents one of the few unfortunate examples in the Upper Midwest of how enthusiasm, misunderstanding, and failure to protect can damage priceless cultural monuments. The park is one of the most popular in the state, and the number of visitors every year is vast, doing great damage to the unfenced effigy mounds that have been here for nearly a thousand years. At last visit, no upgrading of the park site had been undertaken or any kind of educational signage to help the visitor understand the sacredness of the site, all a great loss for the national cultural inheritance. High Cliff State Park does offer a full range of recreational amenities, including hiking and nature trails and a nature center on the grounds.

High Cliff State Park

N7630 State Park Road

Sherwood, WI 54169

920-989-1106

www.dnearstate.wi.us/org/land/parks/specific/highcliff/
index.html

Directions: *From Appleton and Neenah-Menasha:* Take U.S. 10/114 east to Highway 114 south, turn south on Highway 55, and watch for the park entrance sign.

Hours: Open daily.

Helpful Contacts

Calumet County Tourism

P.O. Box 24

Chilton, WI 53014

888-576-9196

www.calumetcountytourism.com

(70) TOFT POINT

Near Bailey's Harbor, WI

Door County is a world apart, bearing an inheritance of rich cultural and ethnic weavings from prehistoric and historic times, right down to the present. More than that, it is a distinct bioenvironment, being a long peninsula surrounded by a bay and an inland sea, experiencing unique currents and winds, migrations, and landforms. At the very tip of "The Door" are an extraordinary biopreserve and an island. The preserve is Toft Point, left virtually undisturbed for a thousand years. The island is called Washington, and it has been home to ancient peoples for an equally long time.

Toft Point is owned by the University of Wisconsin–Green Bay and the Wisconsin Chapter of the Nature Conservancy, which hold it in trust as a unique bioenvironment for the people of Wisconsin. Continuous research is undertaken to better understand and explore the immense diversity of natural plant life here and the ecology of the environment that sustains such life.

A quiet secret of Toft Point is the several groupings of high burial mounds to be found along the drive through the point in the meadows between the road and the lakeshore. Though a few are sheltered by trees, most can easily be seen from the car. These are among the few mounds known in Wisconsin that are not sited in the classic high ground above water: Lake Michigan's tides are barely discernible and unlikely to ever encroach on the mounds.

Do stay in the area for the day and visit the wonderful Ridges Sanctuary in the village of Bailey's Harbor.

Toft Point, State Natural Area No. 57

Point Drive
Bailey's Harbor, WI 54202
www.dnearstate.wi.us/org/land/ER/SNAS/SNAS57.HTM
Directions: *From Bailey's Harbor:* Take State Highway 57 into town, turn onto Ridges Road, and drive east on Ridges Road and then east on Point Drive. The mounds will be on the right off the road. If you wish, you can continue on Point Drive to the end of the peninsula.

Helpful Contacts

Door County Chamber of Commerce
1015 Green Bay Road, P.O. Box 406

Sturgeon Bay, WI 54235

920-743-4456 or 800-527-3529

info@doorcounty.com

http://doorcounty.com

(71) WASHINGTON ISLAND MOUNDS

Washington Island, WI

Washington Island, lying off the point of the peninsula, has been home to many early peoples, most recently to the Ho-Chunk (Winnebago) and the Potawatomi. Many of the small harborages have small conical mounds along the roadsides, hiding—as it were—in plain sight. This is just another lovely reason to visit one of the most delightful places in the entire Upper Midwest.

Directions: *From the peninsula mainland:* The Washington Island Ferry makes regular runs throughout the year, with greatly expanded scheduling in the summer months.

Helpful Contacts

Door County Chamber of Commerce

1015 Green Bay Road, P.O. Box 406

Sturgeon Bay, WI 54235

920-743-4456 or 800-527-3529

info@doorcounty.com

http://doorcounty.com

Washington Island Ferry

www.wisferry.com

(72) COPPER CULTURE STATE PARK AND MUSEUM
Oconto, WI

This 48-acre park shelters a 2,000-year-old Copper Culture burial ground (Late Archaic) found on a bank above the Oconto ("plentiful with fish") River just west of where the river flows into Lake Michigan. Unlike other archaeology park sites in this guide, Copper Culture State Park represents a tradition of pit burials rather than mounds to conceal the dead. Excavation in the 1950s revealed that the pits contained the oldest known forged copper tools yet discovered in North America, including axe heads, spear points, harpoons, knives, fishhooks, and ornaments.

The Copper Culture burial ground is on the west side of Oconto. A small museum is just nearby with exhibits and artifacts on the Copper Culture era. The park has picnic facilities and nature trails.

Copper Culture State Park and Museum
Mill Street
Oconto, WI 54153
920-492-5836
www.ocontocountyhistsoc.org/copper_culture_state_park.htm
Directions: Take U.S. 41 into Oconto, turn west on Highway 22, turn left again on Mott Street, and bear left onto Mill Street and the park entrance.

Helpful Contacts

Oconto County Visitors Bureau
888-626-6862
www.ocontocounty.org

(73) ADVENTURE COPPER MINE

Near Greenland, MI

The last stop on our tour of Upper Midwest archaeology parks takes us out of Wisconsin altogether and up into Michigan's Copper Country in the Upper Peninsula. The Adventure Copper Mine, a modern name for an ancient Copper Culture site, exists to give visitors an understanding of the earliest known copper-mining techniques in this part of the world.

The hard-hat guided tour takes visitors down into the mine to demonstrate the ancient methods of mining used as early as 3,000 B.C.E. and to share suggestions for the disappearance of this ancient people around 1,200 B.C.E. An aboveground walking tour continues the discussion of prehistoric mining techniques and then moves into consideration of historic times up to the 1930s. A jacket and walking shoes are recommended. There is a bookshop on the premises, and there are camping sites on the property; reservations are requested.

Adventure Copper Mine

200 Adventure Road, P.O. Box 6

Greenland, MI 49929

906-883-3371

www.exploringthenorth.com/mine/venture.html

Directions: *From Eagle River, WI:* Take U.S. 45 north into Michigan to Highway 38 (Greenland Road), turn left and drive past the Highway 26 intersection to the first left turn, connect to Adventure Road, and watch for the sign. *From Ironwood, MI:* Take U.S. 2 to Highway 28 east, to Highway 26 north, and to Highway 38 (Greenland Road); take the next left turn, connect to

Adventure Road, and watch for the sign.

Hours: Open daily from Memorial Day through mid-October.

Helpful Contacts

Western U.P. Convention and Visitor Bureau
P.O. Box 706
Ironwood, MI 49938-0706
906-932-4850
bigsnow@westernup.com
www.westernup.com/history

HELPFUL CONTACTS

Planning a heritage travel itinerary requires detailed information from a great many sources. This book helps you plan visits to the parks of interest to you; and the many noted state and county historical societies, state tourism and county chamber of commerce offices, and local and regional interest groups can help you add other places of interest around the parks listed in this book and also help you decide where you would like to stay. The Internet can offer you most of the listings you need, and your public library offers excellent regional and state travel guides for your assistance.

NATIONAL PARK SERVICE

National Park Service
1849 C Street, N.W.
Washington, DC 20240
202-208-6843
www.nps.gov

Midwest Region

National Park Service
1709 Jackson Street

Omaha, NE 68102

402-221-3471

STATE OF MINNESOTA

Minnesota Historical Society and Minnesota State Historic Preservation Office

345 West Kellogg Boulevard

St. Paul, MN 55102

651-296-6126 or 800-657-3773

www.mnhs.org

Minnesota State Parks

Department of Natural Resources Information Center

500 Lafayette Road

St. Paul, MN 55155-4040

651-296-6157 or 888-MINNDNR

www.dnearstate.mn.us

Minnesota Office of Tourism

100 Metro Square, 121 7th Place East

St. Paul, MN 55101

651-296-5029 or 800-657-3700

explore@state.mn.us

www.exploreminnesota.com

Minnesota Office of the State Archaeologist

Fort Snelling History Center

St. Paul, MN 55111-4061

612-725-2411

www.admin.state.mn.us/osa

Science Museum of Minnesota

120 West Kellogg Boulevard

St. Paul, MN 55102

651-221-9444

info@smm.org

www.smm.org

STATE OF IOWA

State Historical Society of Iowa and the Iowa State Historic Preservation Office

www.iowahistory.org

Museum

State of Iowa Historical Building

600 East Locust

Des Moines, IA 50319-0290

515-281-5111

Archives and Collections

State Historical Society of Iowa

Centennial Building

402 Iowa Avenue

Iowa City, IA 52240-1806

319-335-3916

Iowa State Parks

Iowa Department of Natural Resources

502 East 9th Street, Wallace State Office Building

Des Moines, IA 50319-0034

515-281-5918

www.state.ia.us/dnr/organiza/ppd

Iowa Tourism Office

200 East Grand Avenue

Des Moines, IA 50309

515-242-4705 or 888-472-6035

www.traveliowa.com

Iowa Office of the State Archaeologist

University of Iowa

700 Clinton Street Building

Iowa City, IA 52242

319-384-0732

osa@uiowa.edu

STATE OF ILLINOIS

Illinois State Historical Society

210 1/2 South Sixth

Springfield, IL 62701-1503

217-525-2781

www.historyillinois.org

Illinois State Parks

Illinois Department of Natural Resources

Office of Land Management and Education

One Natural Resources Way

Springfield, IL 62702-1271

217-782-6752

http://dnearstate.il.us/lands/landmgt/parks

Illinois Office of Tourism

800-2CONNECT

Tourism@illinoisbiz.biz

www.enjoyillinois.com

Illinois State Museum
Spring and Edwards Streets
Springfield, IL 62706-5000
217-782-7387
www.museum.state.il.us

Ilinois State Historic Preservation Office and Illinois Office of the State Archaeologist

Union Station
500 East Madison Street
Springfield, IL 62701
217-785-4512
www.state.il.us/hpa/default.htm

The Field Museum
1400 South Lake Shore Drive
Chicago, IL 60605-2496
312-922-9410
www.fmnh.org

STATE OF WISCONSIN

Wisconsin Historical Society
www.wisconsinhistory.org
Museum and Collections
816 State Street
Madison, WI 53706
608-264-6400

Wisconsin State Historic Preservation Office
608-264-6500

Wisconsin Office of the State Archaeologist

608-264-6495

Wisconsin State Parks

608-266-2181

www.dnearstate.wi.us/org/land/parks

Wisconsin Tourism

201 West Washington Avenue

P.O. Box 7976

Madison, WI 53707-7976

608-266-2161 or 800-432-8747

www.travelwisconsin.com

Logan Museum of Anthropology

Beloit College

College Street and Bushnell Street

Beloit, WI 53511

608-363-2677

www.beloit.edu/~museum/logan

Milwaukee Public Museum

800 West Wells Street

Milwaukee, WI 53233

414-278-2702

www.mpm.edu

TRIBAL NATIONS

Ho-Chunk Nation

Tribal Office Building

W9814 Airport Road

Black River Falls, WI 54615

715-284-9343 or 800-294-9343
http://ho-chunknation.com

Mdewakanton Dakota Community
1351 Sibley Memorial Highway, P.O. Box 50835
Mendota, MN 55150
651-452-4141
www.mendotadakota.org

Iowa Nation
R.R. 1, Box 721
Perkins, OK 74059
405-547-2402 or 888-336 4692
www.iowanation.org

Mille Lacs Band of Ojibwe
43408 Odena Drive
Onamia, MN 56359
320-532-4181
www.millelacsojibwe.org

RESEARCH RESOURCES

Mississippi Valley Archaeology Center
University of Wisconsin–La Crosse
1725 State Street
La Crosse, WI 54601
608-785-8463
www.uwlax.edu/mvac

Institute for Minnesota Archaeology
www.imnarch.org

Upper Midwest Rock Art Research Association

www.tcinternet.net/users/cbailey/index.htm

Minnesota State University–Mankato E-Museum

http://emuseum.mnsu.edu/index.shtml

FURTHER READING

These books can be found at your libraries and state historical societies, ordered through your local bookstores, or purchased directly from their publishers. Website addresses are listed after the publisher name. An excellent source of books and videos on the topic of rock art—regional, national, and international—is Piedra Pintada Books, an e-retailer: www.rock-art.com/books.

Birmingham, Robert A., and Leslie Eisenberg. *Indian Mounds of Wisconsin*. Madison: State Historical Society of Wisconsin, 2000. Contact: 608-264-6565, www.wisconsinhistory.org/publications/index.html

Birmingham, Robert A., and Katherine H. Rankin. *Native American Mounds in Madison and Dane County*. Madison Heritage Publication Series. Madison: City of Madison and State Historical Society of Wisconsin, 1996. Contact: Madison Historic Preservation Landmarks Commission, 608-266-6552, krankin@ci.madison.wi.us

Boszhardt, Robert "Ernie." *Dark Zone Rock Art in Southwestern Wisconsin*. St. Paul: Prairie Smoke Press, 2003. Contact: www.prairiesmokepress.com

Budak, Michael. *Grand Mound*. Minnesota Historic Site Series.

St. Paul: Minnesota Historical Society, 1995. Contact: www.mnhs.org/market/mhspress/new.html

Callahan, Kevin L. *The Jeffers Petroglyphs: Native American Rock Art on the Midwestern Plains*. St. Paul: Prairie Smoke Press, 2001. Contact: www.prairiesmokepress.com

Conway, Thor, and Julie Conway. *Spirits on Stone: The Agawa Pictographs*. Heritage Discoveries, Inc., 1990. Contact: Piedra Pintada Books, www.rock-art.com/books

Dewdney, Selwyn, and Kenneth Kidd. *Indian Rock Paintings of the Great Lakes*. Toronto: University of Toronto Press, for the Quetico Foundation, 1962.

Furtman, Michael. *Magic on the Rocks: Canoe Country Pictographs*. Duluth, Minn.: Birch Portage Press, 2000. Contact: www.michaelfurtman.com/magic.htm

Highsmith, Hugh. *The Mounds of Koshkonong and Rock River*. Fort Atkinson, Wisc.: Highsmith Press, 1997. Contact: Hoard Historical Museum, Fort Atkinson, 920-563-7769, www.hoardmuseum.org

Holliday, Diane Young, and Bobbie Malone. *Digging and Discovery: Wisconsin Archaeology*. Madison: State Historical Society of Wisconsin, 1997. Contact: 608-264-6565, www.wisconsinhistory.org/publications/index.html

Lapham, Increase A. *The Antiquities of Wisconsin, as Surveyed and Described by I. A. Lapham, Civil Engineer, etc*. Washington, D.C.: Smithsonian Institution, for the American Antiquarian Society, 1855; reprinted by Madison: State Historical Society of Wisconsin, 2001. Contact: 608-264-6565, www.wisconsinhistory.org/publications/index.html

Rajnovich, Grace. *Reading Rock Art: Interpreting the Indian Rock Paintings of the Canadian Shield*. Ontario: Natural Heritage/Natural History Inc., 2002 (1994).

Salzer, Robert J., and Grace Rajnovich. *The Gottschall Rockshelter: An Ideological Mystery*. St. Paul: Prairie Smoke Press, 2000. Contact: www.prairiesmokepress.com

Winchell, Newton H., and Theodore H. Lewis. *The Aborigines of Minnesota*. St. Paul: Minnesota Historical Society, 1911.

PARK SITES BY STATE

ILLINOIS

Albany Mounds State Historic Site

Beattie Park Mounds, Rockford

Briscoe Mounds, near Channahon

Higginbotham Woods Forest Preserve, Joliet

Oakwood Cemetery, Joliet

Winfield Mounds Forest Preserve

IOWA

Bellevue State Park

Catfish Creek State Preserve, Mines of Spain Recreation Area,
    near Dubuque

Effigy Mounds National Monument, near Marquette

Fish Farm Mounds State Preserve, near New Albin

Indian Fish Trap State Preserve, near Amana

James Weed Park, Muscatine

Little Maquoketa River Mounds State Preserve, near Dubuque

Pike's Peak State Park, near McGregor

Slinde Mounds State Preserve, near Hanover

Toolesboro Mounds State Preserve

Turkey River Mounds State Preserve

Wickiup Hill Outdoor Learning Center, near Cedar Rapids

MICHIGAN

Adventure Copper Mine, Greenland

MINNESOTA

Cut Foot Sioux Trail, Chippewa National Forest

Grand Mound, near International Falls

Gull Lake Dam

Historic Murphy's Landing, Minnesota Valley National Wildlife
    Refuge, near Shakopee

Indian Mounds Regional Park, St. Paul

Itasca State Park

Jeffers Petroglyphs

Memorial Park, Shakopee

Mille Lacs Kathio State Park

Mounds Springs Park, Minnesota Valley National Wildlife
    Refuge, Bloomington

Pipestone National Monument

Red Wing Archaeological Preserve, Cannon Valley Trail, Red
    Wing

Winnibigoshish Lake Dam, Chippewa National Forest

ONTARIO (CANADA)

Kay Nah Chi Wah Nung, near Rainy River

WISCONSIN

Aztalan State Park, near Lake Mills

Beloit College Mounds

Bird (or Bow and Arrow) Petroform, near Hager City

Birkmose Park, Hudson

Calumet County Park, near Stockbridge

Carroll College Mounds, Waukesha

Copper Culture State Park and Museum, Oconto

Cranberry Creek Mound Group, near Necedah

Cutler Park, Waukesha

Devil's Lake State Park, near Baraboo

Gee's Slough (New Lisbon) Mounds

Henschel Homestead/Museum of Indian History, near Elkhart
    Lake

High Cliff State Park, near Sherwood

Horicon Marsh, near Mayville

Indian Burial Ground, near Spooner

Indian Mounds Park, Rice Lake

Indian Mounds Park, Sheboygan

Indian Mounds Park, Whitewater

Jefferson County Indian Mounds and Trail Park, Koshkonong
    Mounds Country Club, near Fort Atkinson

Kingsley Bend Mounds, near Wisconsin Dells

Lake Emily County Park, Amherst Junction

Lake Kegonsa State Park, near Stoughton

Lakeside Park, Avoca

Lizard Mounds County Park, near West Bend

Madison Mounds District

- The Arboretum
- Burrows Park
- Cherokee Park
- Edgewood College Campus
- Edna Taylor Conservancy
- Elmside Park
- Forest Hill Cemetery
- Goodland County Park
- Governor Nelson State Park
- Hudson Park

- Indian Mound Park
- Mendota State Hospital Grounds
- Observatory Hill
- Picnic Point
- Siggelkow Park
- Spring Harbor School Grounds
- Vilas Circle Park
- Vilas Park
- Willow Drive
- Yahara Heights County Park

Man Mound County Park, near Baraboo

Mound Cemetery, Racine

Myrick Park, La Crosse

Nelson Dewey State Park

Panther Intaglio, Fort Atkinson

Perrot State Park, near Trempealeau

Riverside Cemetery, near Genoa

Roche-A-Cri State Park, near Friendship

Toft Point, near Bailey's Harbor

Upper Whiting Park

Wakanda Park, Menomonie

Washington Island Mounds

Whistler Indian Mounds Park, Hancock

Wisconsin Heights Battle Site, near Sauk City

Wyalusing State Park, near Prairie du Chien

INDEX

ABOUT THE
AUTHOR

Deborah Morse-Kahn is a Minneapolis-based regional historian, author, and editor with a specialization in studies of the Upper Midwest.

1 Grand Mound, near International Falls
2 Kay Nah Chi Wah Nung, Manitou Mounds
3 Cut Foot Sioux Trail, Chippewa National Forest
4 Winnibigoshish Lake Dam, Chippewa National Forest
5 Itasca State Park
6 Gull Lake Dam
7 Mille Lacs Kathio State Park
8 Indian Mounds Regional Park, St. Paul
9 Mounds Springs Park, Bloomington
10 Historic Murphy's Landing, Shakopee
11 Memorial Park, Shakopee
12 Birkmose Park, Hudson
13 Red Wing Archaeological Preserve, Red Wing
14 Bird (or Bow and Arrow) Petroform, near Hager City

15 Indian Burial Ground, near Spooner
16 Indian Mounds Park, Rice Lake
17 Wakanda Park, Menomonie
18 Jeffers Petroglyphs
19 Pipestone National Monument
20 Perrot State Park, near Trempealeau
21 W Myrick Park, La Crosse
22 Riverside Cemetery, near Genoa
23 Fish Farm Mounds State Preserve, near New Albin
24 Slinde Mounds State Preserve, near Hanover
25 Effigy Mounds National Monument
26 Pike's Peak State Park
27 Wyalusing State Park
28 Nelson Dewey State Park

29 Turkey River Mounds State Preserve
30 Little Maquoketa River Mounds State Preserve
31 Catfish Creek State Preserve, Mines of Spain Recreation Area
32 Bellevue State Park
33 Wickiup Hill Outdoor Learning Center, near Cedar Rapids
34 Indian Fish Trap State Preserve, near Amana
35 Toolesboro Mounds State Preserve
36 James Weed Park, Muscatine
37 Albany Mounds State Historic Site
38 Briscoe Mounds, near Channahon
39 Oakwood Cemetery, Joliet
40 Higginbotham Woods Forest Preserve, Joliet
41 Winfield Mounds Forest Preserve
42 Beattie Park Mounds, Rockford

43 Beloit College Mounds
44 Mound Cemetery, Racine
45 Indian Mounds Park, Whitewater
46 Carroll College Mounds, Waukesha
47 Cutler Park, Waukesha
48 Jefferson County Indian Mounds and Trail Park, Koshkonong Mounds C.C., near Fort Atkinson
49 Panther Intaglio, Fort Atkinson
50 Aztalan State Park
51 Lake Kegonsa State Park